ANIMAL PLANET

COMPLETE GUIDE TO
PUPPY CARE

Everything you need
to know to have a
happy, healthy,
well-trained
puppy

tfh

STACY KENNEDY

COMPLETE GUIDE TO PUPPY CARE

Project Team
Editors: Heather Russell-Revesz
Indexer: Dianne L. Schneider
Designer: Mary Ann Kahn

TFH Publications®
President/CEO: Glen S. Axelrod
Executive Vice President: Mark E. Johnson
Publisher: Christopher T. Reggio
Production Manager: Kathy Bontz

TFH Publications, Inc.®
One TFH Plaza
Third and Union Avenues
Neptune City, NJ 07753

Discovery Communications, LLC. Book Development Team: Marjorie Kaplan, President and General Manager, Animal Planet Media/ Kelly Day, Executive Vice President and General Manager, Discovery Commerce/ Elizabeth Bakacs, Vice President, Licensing and Creative/ JP Stoops, Director, Licensing/ Mindy Barsky, Design Director, Licensing/ Bridget Stoyko, Associate Art Director, Licensing

 ©2012 Discovery Communications, LLC. Animal Planet and the Animal Planet logo are trademarks of Discovery Communications, LLC, used under license. All rights reserved. *animalplanet.com*

Printed and bound in China
12 13 14 15 16 17   1 3 5 7 9 8 6 4 2

Derived from *The Simple Guide to Puppies,* originally published in 2000

Library of Congress Cataloging-in-Publication Data
Kennedy, Stacy.
  Complete guide to puppy care : everything you need to know to have a happy, healthy, well-trained puppy / Stacy Kennedy.
      p. cm. -- (Animal planet)
  "Derived from The simple guide to puppies, originally published in 2000"--T.p. verso.
  Includes index.
  ISBN 978-0-7938-3727-4 (alk. paper)
 1. Puppies--Selection--Handbooks, manuals, etc. 2. Puppies--Training. 3. Puppies--Health and hygiene. 4. Puppies--Behavior. I. Kennedy, Stacy. Simple guide to puppies. II. Title.
  SF427.K372 2011
  636.7'07--dc23
                        2011024763

This book has been published with the intent to provide accurate and authoritative information in regard to the subject matter within. While every reasonable precaution has been taken in preparation of this book, the author and publisher expressly disclaim responsibility for any errors, omissions, or adverse effects arising from the use or application of the information contained herein. The techniques and suggestions are used at the reader's discretion and are not to be considered a substitute for veterinary care. If you suspect a medical problem consult your veterinarian.

Note: In the interest of concise writing, "he" is used when referring to puppies and dogs unless the text is specifically referring to females or males. "She" is used when referring to people. However, the information contained herein is equally applicable to both sexes.

PART ONE

GETTING

STARTED

1

SHOULD YOU GET A PUPPY?

So, you are thinking about getting a puppy. Dog ownership is a big step—bigger than most people realize. That adorable little puppy you bring home will mature to become a fully grown adult and will most likely be a member of your family for 12 to 15 years—perhaps even longer.

You will be responsible for your dog's well-being for quite some time. You will also be responsible for training your dog to become well-adjusted and polite, a pleasure to own, and an asset to the neighborhood. You will have to feed, exercise, groom, and keep your pup safe and healthy for life. If it sounds like a major commitment,

Puppies are like babies—adorable and helpless.

it is. Most people do not consider the extent of commitment that dog ownership entails before picking up the first adorable pup they see.

But puppy ownership can be a joy as well. The fulfillment that you receive watching your pup grow and learn is incomparable, as is experiencing the love and affection that a dog gives back in return. Studies have shown that dogs can lower stress, help keep you fit, provide companionship, elicit laughter, and generally improve the quality of your life. By evaluating your needs first and then finding a puppy who best matches those needs, you can ensure that the dog you pick will fit perfectly within your family. Take the time to ask yourself and your family some questions about your

lifestyle and what you all want to see in a dog. Then do your research. When you find the "perfect" puppy who will be your companion for life, you'll be glad you did.

DO YOU HAVE THE TIME?

Puppies are like babies—absolutely adorable but also pretty helpless. Bringing an eight- or ten-week-old puppy into your home is almost like bringing a newborn home from the hospital; the "baby" will need your utmost attention and time until you both settle into a routine. For a few days, the puppy might be a little scared and lonely without the company of his mom and littermates. The pup will need extra attention and assurance until these new surroundings become familiar.

You will need to establish a schedule for eating, drinking, and outdoor time. Successful housetraining depends on a schedule. Puppies need to be taken to their potty area every few hours until they are at least 16 weeks of age (older for females), at which time they have better control of their bodily functions. They also need to go potty after eating, drinking, napping, and playing, as well as first thing in the morning and last thing at night.

Once housetrained, your puppy will still need to go outside at least three times a day, as well as get regular exercise to burn off all of that exuberant puppy energy. You'll need to spend time training; at first, to teach your puppy the household rules, and then good manners and basic obedience. You'll also need to spend time on grooming and on socializing him by going places,

meeting people, and adjusting to different situations. That's a lot of time you'll need to spend with your new addition.

If you work ten-hour days or travel a lot and no one else is home to care for the dog, there is no way you will be able to give your puppy enough attention. This is completely unfair and will result in an unhappy and destructive puppy, which, in turn, will make your life miserable. Be fair—if you and your family do not have the time to spend, don't bring a puppy into your life!

HOW MUCH SPACE?

Dogs, even small ones, need space— space to play, grow, exercise, and be alone when they want. The amount of space you can provide will determine what kind of dog is best for you—or help you to rethink dog ownership.

First, there are basic considerations: Are you allowed to have a dog in your residence? If you rent your home or apartment or live in restricted housing like a condominium complex or retirement village, you may not be permitted to have a dog. Check your lease or your community by-laws to confirm that dogs are allowed in your home before investing your time and money in a puppy.

If you are permitted to have a dog or if you own your residence, take inventory of the space available. If you live in an apartment or condo, make sure that it is possible for you to take your puppy out for frequent walks and potty breaks. If your dog has access to a yard, is that yard fenced? Will your dog have

Consider how much grooming your puppy will need as an adult.

unlimited access to the yard or will you need to build a dog run? Remember that your well-tended garden can be dug up in no time by an industrious young puppy who wants to "help" you plant the spring flower beds. Building your puppy a dog run or designated area to use may be the best way to keep your yard looking nice. All of these things need to be considered before you bring a new puppy home.

Consider the size of your residence. A giant breed like a Great Dane or a Saint Bernard will not be happy or comfortable in a studio apartment, and a little dog may feel overwhelmed with free access to a large house. Choose a puppy who will "fit in" best, especially when he is a full-sized adult.

What about your furnishings? Although they don't do it intentionally, puppies can be destructive. No matter how careful you

are about trying to prevent it, little puppy teeth often find their way onto table legs and through couch cushions. Puppies will also have accidents on nice rugs, spill water on floors, and track mud through hallways. If a pristine house is really important to you, then you might think twice before getting a puppy.

WHAT IS YOUR LIFESTYLE?

As previously stated, one of the most important factors to consider before choosing a puppy is the opinions of all the members of the household. Everyone who lives in your home must want a puppy. Even if you're sure you want a puppy to join the family, the type of dog you choose will be dependent on the dynamics of the household. A puppy can be successfully raised in all types of family situations—it's just a matter of finding the right puppy for each situation. Every dog, no matter what size, energy level, coat type, or exercise requirements, can find a family for a perfect fit.

For example, a senior couple may want to choose a puppy who will grow to be a small adult—one who can be easily handled and who may not need as much exercise as a larger dog. A household with small children may want a dog with a tolerant personality and good disposition, while a household with older children may want a dog who can match their high level of energy and play. A single person or couple with no children may want a dog who is more independent, rather than one who likes to run in packs. Some people may even

consider getting two dogs to keep each other company.

It is important to research the different breeds as much as possible; get to know the breeds' personalities, talk to people who own them, and visit and play with the dogs before taking one home. Most dogs are placed in shelters because of behavior and training problems that could have been solved by better research beforehand and more time put into the training program. The more time and energy you put into finding the right dog, the more heartbreak you'll save yourself and your family. Just as in human families, individuals within a breed are not

When you are choosing which breed of puppy you want, coat type is a very important consideration. Different breeds have different types of coats, and each will have specific grooming requirements. Don't get me wrong—every dog, purebred or mixed breed, needs regular grooming to stay healthy and look his best. But how regular is regular? Do you want to spend lots of time every day on grooming, or will your schedule only permit once a week? If you choose a breed that requires clipping, trimming, or stripping, are you willing to learn or would you rather pay someone to do it for you? Does shedding really bother you? The answers to these questions can be important factors when choosing a breed.

all alike. Remember to evaluate the individual dog as well as the breed.

All breeds need some type of grooming.

HOW MUCH GROOMING?

As dogs evolved through the ages, each group developed coats for protection from both the elements and predators. As dogs were selectively bred for certain purposes, their coats became matters of function. Dogs with short, smooth coats were good hunters because they didn't pick up burrs or become stuck in the field. Long coats helped dogs who were bred to work in colder climates stay warm. Through selective breeding by humans, dogs developed coats for specialized purposes, and although a good number of modern-day dogs are house pets, they still retain the coat that was best for their original function.

Coat Types

We'll discuss the coats of specific breeds in a later chapter, but the following list will give you a general idea of coat types:

- **Curly or Short, Wavy Coats:** Poodles, Irish Water Spaniels, Kerry Blue Terriers, Portuguese Water Dogs
- **Wire Coats:** Most Terriers, All Schnauzers
- **Long Coats:** Rough Collies, Australian Shepherds, Shetland Sheepdogs, Lhasa Apsos, Most Spaniels
- **Silky Coats:** Afghan Hounds, Yorkshire Terriers, Irish, English, and Gordon Setters
- **Smooth Coats:** Doberman Pinschers, Boxers, Great Danes, Beagles, Basset Hounds, Dalmatians
- **Short Coats:** Labrador Retrievers, German Shepherd Dogs, Welsh Corgis (Pembroke and Cardigan)

HOW ACTIVE ARE YOU?

All healthy puppies are playful, active, and full of energy. Puppies do grow up, however, and each breed will have certain exercise requirements that must be regularly met for its physical and mental well-being. If you pick the right puppy, the level of activity that both of you enjoy should be a perfect match throughout your life together.

What activities do you and your family participate in? Which of these activities can your dog join? The answers to these questions can play a big part in determining the kind of dog you want. A jogger may want an active dog with a lot of stamina and energy. A swimmer or a boater may want a dog who loves the water. A hunter may want a dog to participate in field events. You may want to try your hand at obedience, agility, herding trials, earthdog events, lure coursing, flyball, or any other activities that you can do with your dog, or you may just want a dog who fits your mellow personality. If your idea of exercise is a couple of quick walks around the block, a short-legged Dachshund, a low-energy Bulldog, or a sauntering Saint Bernard may be the right breed for you. However, if you jog 5 miles (8 km) every day and hike on the weekends, an active retriever or a high-energy Australian Shepherd or Border Collie may suit your needs.

Picking the breed with the right activity level will keep both dog and owner happy.

> Each breed will have certain exercise requirements that must be regularly met.

The right mix can be met to keep everyone involved (dog and human) physically and mentally fit. The dog's exercise needs will be met, which will keep your pet from becoming bored or overweight, and you will have a lifelong companion who is fun to take wherever you go. Remember, proper exercise will not only keep your dog looking good, it will keep you in shape as well.

2

WHICH PUPPY IS RIGHT FOR YOU?

Now that you've answered some important questions about your lifestyle, it's time to find out a little about what kinds of dog are out there. The answer is...plenty! There is literally a dog for every owner if you do your research. The best thing to do is narrow down the field to a few breeds that have the characteristics you find desirable and then read as much about them as possible. There are many good, detailed books that give the histories and characteristics of each breed, as well as show pictures that illustrate exactly what the dog should look like. If you are interested in adopting a dog, read as much about the process as possible. The better educated you are, the better your chances of finding the perfect puppy for you.

THE PUREBRED DOG

There are certain advantages to choosing a purebred puppy. First, a purebred offers you a guarantee of what your puppy will look like as an adult—the size, coat type, activity level, and natural instincts have all been passed down from generation to generation. Second, because you are more likely to meet and observe the mother of your puppy, temperament can be better evaluated. When looking for a purebred dog of any breed, it is very important to find a responsible breeder who has been recommended by her national breed club. This way, you are assured that breeders will breed only the best dogs and that their dogs have been certified free of certain heritable, genetic diseases. (How to find a breeder is discussed later in this book.)

If you want a purebred puppy but don't know what breed would be best for your family, look for an online dog breed selector test. There are many of these tests on the web, and they typically prompt you through a series of questions and then put together a list of breeds that may be right for you. Many sites show pictures of each breed and give you information on size, activity level, trainability, temperament, and grooming requirements. One you might want to try is at www.selectsmart.com.

The American Kennel Club (AKC) recognizes 167 breeds of dog as of this printing, and there are more than 400 breeds recognized worldwide. The breeds recognized by the AKC are divided into seven groups, which were derived from each breed's origin and purpose. The most popular dogs from each group are featured in the following galleries.

THE HERDING GROUP

Breeds in the Herding Group have been an integral part of every country's use of livestock, and the herding dog still retains many of the physical characteristics and instincts for this work. The herding breeds have been bred to be intelligent, athletic, and diligent and are arguably the most trainable of all breeds—making them naturals for obedience work, agility, and herding trials. Throughout the years, responsible breeders have perpetuated the herding dogs' natural instincts. They have evolved into independent but loyal dogs who are happiest when at work serving their owners. As long as they get enough exercise and mental stimulation, herding dogs can make wonderful, devoted pets who will thrive on (and demand) your companionship.

TOP AKC HERDING GROUP BREEDS

Australian Cattle Dog
These dogs have two speeds: extremely fast and comatose.

Australian Shepherd
Aussies are smart, friendly, and full of energy.

Belgian Malinois
The Malinois is one of four Belgian sheepdogs, all of whom are intelligent and driven.

Border Collie

Border Collies have intense drive and high intelligence.

Bouvier des Flandres

This powerful breed has served as a rough-coated cattle dog.

Cardigan Welsh Corgi

Corgis are watchful and devoted.

TOP AKC HERDING GROUP BREEDS

Collie
This noble breed is exemplified by the famous character Lassie.

German Shepherd Dog
The GSD is one of the most versatile dogs in the world.

Icelandic Sheepdog
This herding dog's sense of smell is legendary.

Old English Sheepdog
The "Bobtail" is protective
yet gentle.

Pembroke Welsh Corgi
Corgis can make good watchdogs
and are devoted to their families.

Shetland Sheepdog
Shelties are lively but gentle.

THE HOUND GROUP

There is little doubt that a hound-type dog was one of the earliest breeds that existed. Hounds were used in ancient times to hunt animals. While times have changed and few hounds today are used for hunting purposes, this instinct remains strong in all the breeds in this group. The hounds are divided into two subgroups: the sighthounds and the scenthounds; the eyesight of the sighthound is excellent and the scenting ability of the scenthound is very keen. These hounds were selectively bred to hunt a wide variety of animals. Sighthounds were used to find and chase down large game such as deer, elk, moose, and wild boar. Medium-sized hounds used both sight and scent for smaller game like rabbits and foxes. Small hounds used scent to chase prey into the ground. The Hound Group is diversified; it includes both giant breeds and small breeds and is divided according to how the breed hunts.

TOP AKC HOUND GROUP BREEDS

Afghan Hound
The Afghan Hound is elegant and independent.

Basenji
This breed is smart, inquisitive, and independent-minded.

Basset Hound

This sweet, gentle hound has a deep, melodic voice.

Beagle

Beagles are playful, curious, and self-assured.

Black and Tan Coonhound

This hunter is confident and courageous.

TOP AKC HOUND GROUP BREEDS

Bloodhound
This kind-souled hound is single-minded in the field.

Borzoi
These independent sighthounds are remarkably calm indoors.

Dachshund
Dachshunds are lively, alert, and comic.

Irish Wolfhound
This gentle giant is extremely loyal to his family.

Rhodesian Ridgeback
This strong and brave hunter is very protective of his owners.

Whippet
This easygoing, adaptable breed is gentle and affectionate.

THE NON-SPORTING GROUP

A diverse collection of breeds, the Non-Sporting Group is made up of those dogs who no longer perform the duties for which they were bred. For example, the Dalmatian is no longer used to accompany horse-drawn carriages, and the Bulldog is no longer used for bullbaiting. They have all found a home in the Non-Sporting Group, which is one of the fastest-growing groups in popularity. Included are many popular and well-known breeds that range in size, activity level, coat type, and origin, offering dog owners a choice of breeds to fit every taste.

TOP AKC NON-SPORTING GROUP BREEDS

Bichon Frise
The Bichon is an outgoing, merry, personable dog.

Boston Terrier
Keen, intelligent, and biddable, the Boston is known as the "American Gentleman."

Bulldog
Although extremely gentle, the Bulldog
is protective of his family.

Chinese Shar-Pei
This independent, alert guarding breed
is devoted and loyal.

Chow Chow
Chows tend to bond strongly to
one person.

TOP AKC NON-SPORTING GROUP BREEDS

Dalmatian
This breed has a great deal of energy and enthusiasm.

French Bulldog
Frenchies are playful, inquisitive, and affectionate and make great companions.

Keeshond
This outgoing, family-oriented breed is often called "The Laughing Dutchman."

Lhasa Apso
This friendly, spirited breed is a highly regarded companion.

Poodle
All three sizes of Poodles are lively, intelligent, and active.

Shiba Inu
This agile, independent breed is sometimes described as "cat-like."

TOP AKC NON-SPORTING GROUP BREEDS

Tibetan Terrier
This adaptive, companionable breed makes a great watchdog.

THE SPORTING GROUP

From the 1600s, sporting dogs have been developed to assist hunters in finding, pointing, flushing, holding, and retrieving game. Of the three types of sporting dogs—pointers, setters, and retrievers—many still perform the duties for which they were originally bred. Loyalty to their masters and trainability have helped them to become some of the most popular breeds for families. They have not been confined to using their skills just for hunting. These talented breeds also excel as therapy dogs, assistance dogs, and search and rescue dogs. Athletic and active, they are known for their good natures and enthusiastic attitudes, but they need plenty of exercise to keep their positive outlooks.

TOP AKC SPORTING GROUP BREEDS

Brittany
The Brittany is an intense hunter who is easy to handle and train.

Chesapeake Bay Retriever
The Chessie is a tough, tenacious, exceptional sporting companion.

Cocker Spaniel (American)
This breed is happy, trusting, and gentle.

English Cocker Spaniel
The English Cocker is happy and exuberant.

English Springer Spaniel

The Springer is an even-tempered, merry, affectionate dog.

German Shorthaired Pointer

The GSP is an exuberant, versatile hunting dog.

German Wirehaired Pointer

The GWP is more reserved than his relative, the GSP, but both share the same zeal for hunting.

Golden Retriever

Goldens are lovable and easygoing, and make wonderful family dogs.

Gordon Setter

This steady and honest hunting dog is cheerful and gentle in the home.

Irish Setter

This elegant and athletic setter has an upbeat personality.

TOP AKC SPORTING GROUP BREEDS

Labrador Retriever
The Lab is sensible, even-tempered, affectionate, and willing to please.

Vizsla
The Vizsla is handsome and highly energetic.

Weimaraner
This is a talented, friendly, alert, high-energy dog.

Wirehaired Pointing Griffon
The "Griff" is a wonderful companion for anyone who loves the outdoors.

THE TERRIER GROUP

The name "terrier" is derived from the Latin word *terra*, meaning earth; thus, the terrier is an earth dog. Terrier breeds come in all sizes. Developed specially to go to ground and burrow in the earth to chase and catch vermin like rats, foxes, badgers, weasels, and otters, the terrier was selectively bred for centuries to be a determined and tenacious dog. Long the companions of farmers, they also quickly endeared themselves to city dwellers looking for exterminators. They are the dog world's "tough guys." Although usually friendly with people, they will not back down from an aggressive incident with other dogs, no matter what their size.

Some of the terriers have distinctive double coats, consisting of soft undercoats and wiry jackets that need special grooming. Many are plucked or stripped by hand, which is a time-consuming process that gives them a unique appearance.

TOP AKC TERRIER GROUP BREEDS

Airedale Terrier
The Airedale is brassy, bold, smart, and high-spirited.

American Staffordshire Terrier
Bred and raised properly, the AmStaff is a confident, loving, intelligent companion.

Border Terrier
This small dog has a huge amount of pluck and verve.

Bull Terrier

This intelligent and active breed is very attached to his family.

Cairn Terrier

The Cairn is cheerful, alert, endearing, and independent.

Miniature Schnauzer

This breed is lively, charismatic, rugged, and alert.

TOP AKC TERRIER GROUP BREEDS

Norwich Terrier

One of the smallest of the terriers, the Norwich is sociable yet feisty and full of himself.

Parson Russell Terrier

This bold and athletic terrier is up for any challenge or game.

Scottish Terrier

Scotties are intelligent, courageous, dignified, and loyal.

Soft Coated Wheaten Terrier
The Wheaten is alert, friendly, happy and often quieter than the smaller terriers.

Staffordshire Bull Terrier
Animated and clever, the Staffy Bull has a devoted, playful temperament.

West Highland White Terrier
Westies are charming, hardy, devoted, and spunky.

TOP AKC TERRIER GROUP BREEDS

Wire Fox Terrier
Outgoing, energetic, and self-assured, these terriers make sturdy pets.

THE TOY GROUP

If you are looking for a lot of dog in a small package, a toy breed may be for you. The "toy" part of this breed's name refers to size only. These breeds have such spunk and strong personalities that they often dominate larger dogs, and in some cases, people. Many have descended from larger breeds of terriers or spaniels and still retain those inherent instincts. Others ruled the roost as prized lapdogs and companions to royalty. Despite their small size, they are very vocal defenders of their homes and are ideal pets for those with limited space.

TOP AKC TOY GROUP BREEDS

Cavalier King Charles Spaniel
This sweet, endearing, joyful dog has expressive eyes.

Chihuahua

This lively, alert, affectionate breed has self-confidence way beyond his tiny size.

Chinese Crested

The Chinese Crested may be a bit shy with strangers but is lively, exuberant, playful, and affectionate with those he loves.

Havanese

The responsive, alert, friendly Havanese is a delightful companion.

TOP AKC TOY GROUP BREEDS

Italian Greyhound
Iggies are inquisitive, gentle, fast, and often bond to one person.

Japanese Chin
Chins are happy, playful, mild-mannered toys who love attention.

Maltese
The Maltese is spirited, affectionate, loyal, mischievous, and adorable.

Miniature Pinscher

Curious and fearless, the Min Pin doesn't miss anything that's going on around him.

Papillon

These versatile, intelligent toys are happy dogs at heart.

Pekingese

This breed is full of charm, confidence, and a bit of stubborn independence.

TOP AKC TOY GROUP BREEDS

Pomeranian
The spunky Pom is alert, active, intelligent, and full of himself.

Pug
The Pug is an even-tempered, happy, affectionate, and jovial companion.

Shih Tzu
This breed is a gentle lapdog and a playful companion.

Silky Terrier

The Silky is lively, smart, and friendly, but is less of a lapdog than some other toys.

Toy Fox Terrier

This athletic and sturdy breed is gregarious, friendly, and loves high-energy sports.

Yorkshire Terrier

This charming toy still has plenty of terrier in him —he's feisty, fearless, and ready to take on the world.

THE WORKING GROUP

All domestic dogs were once bred with the purpose of serving humankind, many breeds originally doing specific work for their owners. In every country, breeds were created to be draft dogs, hunters, and guardians. Many continue those duties today. The medium to very large breeds that make up the Working Group are well known for their athleticism, strength, courage, and loyalty—all attributes that have made them invaluable to the people who rely on them. Working dog enthusiasts have been concerned with retaining these breeds' versatility and function along with form. These breeds now often serve as police dogs, search and rescue dogs, therapy dogs, sled dogs, and draft dogs. Because of their large size and protective tendencies, they need proper socialization and training, along with plenty of exercise. If you can provide a working dog with a job to do, you'll have an enthusiastic partner for life.

TOP AKC WORKING GROUP BREEDS

Akita
This breed is fearless, brave, strong, independent, and intelligent.

Alaskan Malamute
This loyal, devoted breed is boisterous and affectionate.

Bernese Mountain Dog
The even-tempered Berner is friendly, easygoing, and alert.

Boxer
This high-energy, athletic dog is curious, playful, and high-spirited.

Bullmastiff
The size and strength of this devoted and alert breed can be intimidating.

TOP AKC WORKING GROUP BREEDS

Cane Corso
This guard dog is intelligent, protective, and devoted to his family.

Doberman Pinscher
Dobies are athletic and powerful, light footed and aristocratic.

Dogue de Bordeaux
Although he's usually a teddy bear with his family, this is a formidable and powerful breed.

Giant Schnauzer

This working dog has a terrier-like temperament—he's bold, spirited, and protective.

Great Dane

Although he is protective toward his family, overall the Great Dane is a playful, affectionate, and patient breed.

Great Pyrenees

This large, intelligent, imposing dog would give his life to protect his flock.

Greater Swiss Mountain Dog

Even-tempered, intelligent, and generally mellow, the Swissy makes a wonderful family dog.

Leonberger

This breed is grand and imposing yet supremely affectionate, patient, and noble.

Mastiff

This exceptional protector is self-confident, patient, steady, and docile.

Newfoundland
The Newfie is the gentlest of giants—he's noble, honest, and devoted to his family.

Portuguese Water Dog
This extremely intelligent, athletic, robust dog is an independent thinker.

Rottweiler
Rotties are protective, attentive, and loyal.

TOP AKC WORKING GROUP BREEDS

Samoyed
The Sammy is exceptionally friendly, easygoing, and affectionate.

Siberian Husky
This tireless breed is friendly, gentle, alert, and independent.

Saint Bernard
Saint Bernards are friendly, patient, loyal, and eager to please.

Standard Schnauzer

This spirited, loyal, intelligent companion excels at many competitive events.

BREEDS IN A NUTSHELL

While every dog is an individual, there are some generalizations we can make about certain breed traits.

The Eager Beavers

Some breeds want nothing more than to please their owners, while others just want to do as they please. A few of the breeds most likely to want to make you happy and therefore train more easily are: Australian Shepherd, Border Collie, Doberman Pinscher, German Shepherd Dog, Golden Retriever, Labrador Retriever, Rottweiler, Shetland Sheepdog, and the Welsh Corgi.

The Exercise Nuts

Some breeds just can't get enough exercise, and need extensive daily workouts. A few of these high-energy breeds include: Australian Cattle Dog, Australian Shepherd, Border Collie, Boxer, Dalmation, Labrador Retriever, Rhodesian Ridgeback, Weimaraner.

The Hair-Raisers

Some coats take a lot more work than others. The breeds that need some extra time on the grooming table include: Afghan Hound, Bichon Frise, Borzoi, Irish Setter, Maltese, Pekingese, Poodle, Portuguese Water Dog, Shih Tzu, Yorkshire Terrier, and many of the terriers.

The Heavyweights

Some breeds are more likely to pudge out than others. If you have one of the following breeds, you should pay special attention to keeping your dog fit and trim: Bulldog, Beagle, Cocker Spaniel, Basset Hound, Dachshund, Labrador Retriever, and Pug.

The Independent Thinkers

Some breeds are independent and prefer to make their own decisions, which makes them harder to train. A few of these breeds include: Afghan Hound, Akita, Chow Chow, Shiba Inu, Siberian Husky, and many of the terriers.

The Tough Guys

Some dogs will back up their bark with a bite. A few of the breeds that exhibit very protective behavior are: Akita, American Staffordshire Terrier, Cane Corso, Doberman Pinscher, Dogue de Bordeaux, German Shepherd Dog, Giant Schnauzer, Mastiff, and Rottweiler.

THE MIXED BREED

Mixed-breed puppies, or "mutts" as they are sometimes affectionately called, can also make great pets. There are thousands of dogs in shelters all around the country who are just waiting to be adopted. Besides being abundant, mixed breeds, because of their varied backgrounds, may escape many of the genetic problems that purebred dogs face. To ensure that you get the best mixed breed for your family situation, find out as much about the puppy's history, background, and former treatment as possible. It also helps to know what breeds make up the "mix" so that you may better gauge the pup's temperament and needs. Having this information can help predict future problems and allow you to formulate a solution if they should arise.

Although mixed breeds cannot compete in AKC organized events, they can be trained to do anything that a purebred can do, including obedience, agility, flyball, search and rescue, and therapy dog programs. Adopting a mixed breed from a shelter will not only provide you with a grateful, lifelong companion, you will have the knowledge that you have saved the life of a special puppy or dog.

WHERE
TO FIND
YOUR PUPPY

3

If you have decided that a purebred dog is right for you, you must first find a reputable breeder. This cannot be stressed enough! It is very important that your puppy be purchased from a breeder who has earned a reputation for consistently producing dogs who are physically healthy and mentally sound. Breeders earn that reputation strictly by breeding their dogs selectively. Selective breeding aims to maintain the virtues of a breed and to eliminate genetic weaknesses.

FINDING A RESPONSIBLE BREEDER

A national breed club can assist a prospective dog buyer in finding a responsible breeder of quality puppies. If you call any of these clubs or log on to their websites, you will find that each national breed club will have the name and address or phone number of a member that can refer you to a reputable breeder in your area.

The responsible breeder will breed for good temperaments and will ensure that her puppies are properly socialized—the socialization process should not be overlooked. Proper socialization will help produce a mentally stable dog who is able to get along with all kinds of people and other animals. A well-socialized puppy will not show fear, shyness, or aggressiveness.

When searching for a breeder, also consider what kinds of activities you'd like to do with your dog. For example, if you want a Chesapeake Bay Retriever for hunting, try to find a breeder who has bred successful and titled hunting dogs.

The breeder should also be able to produce registration papers for

A good breeder will allow you to meet the dam of the litter of puppies.

the mother and the litter, although these documents may be withheld until some conditions are met, such as spaying or neutering the pup.

Signs of a Good Breeder

With any luck, you will be able to find a reputable breeder in your area who will have at least one of the puppy's parents on the premises. Good breeders are willing to have you see the dam (and sire) of the litter, as well as inspect the facility where the dogs are raised. Additionally, a responsible breeder will:

- Keep the puppies until they're at least seven weeks old (most preferably until they are nine weeks).
- Welcome questions and answer them willingly.
- Encourage you to visit and meet her dogs.
- Belong to one or more dog clubs.
- Screen all breeding dogs for inherited diseases. The parents should be certified by the Orthopedic Foundation for Animals (OFA) or PennHip™ as being free of hip dysplasia. The Canine Eye Registration Foundation (CERF) finds animals free of hereditary eye diseases such as cataracts and progressive retinal atrophy in breeds that require such clearance.
- Know the inherited problems that occur

A good breeder will not allow a puppy who is too young to leave his mom and littermates.

in the breed and does not claim that her dogs' bloodlines are free of health problems. (There's no such thing as a "clean line.")

- Require you to spay or neuter your pet puppy.
- Tell you about the challenges of owning the breed.
- Handle and socialize her puppies.
- Keep her dogs in a clean environment.
- Know every adult dog and every puppy as an individual.
- Willingly refer you to her previous buyers.
- Ask for and check your references.
- Provide you with necessary paperwork like inoculation records and pedigree (see Chapter 6 for details) and not charge extra for "papers."
- Not pressure you to buy a puppy; in fact, she'll make you prove you're good enough to own one!

Do not be surprised if a breeder asks lots of questions about you, your family, and the environment in which the puppy will be raised. Good breeders are just as concerned about puppies going to good homes as you are in obtaining a well-adjusted, healthy dog. Breeders will use all of the information you give them to match the right puppy with the right home. Typical questions from a breeder are:

- What breeds have you previously owned?
- What other animals do you own now?
- How much time will you have to devote to a new puppy?
- Do you have a fenced-in yard?
- Do you have children?
- Have you ever surrendered a dog to a shelter or rescue group?
- Do you rent? (If you rent your home, you may be required to show proof that your landlord will allow you to own a dog.)

While this may seem like an interrogation of sorts, keep in mind that these are all legitimate concerns for a breeder who wants the best for her pups.

Most breeders will not allow their puppies to go to their new homes until after they have been given their first vaccinations—usually at about eight weeks of age. Once weaned, your puppy is highly susceptible to many infectious diseases that can be transmitted through people. It is best to make sure your puppy is inoculated before leaving the breeder's residence. You should continue the immunization schedule with your veterinarian.

Non-Local Breeders

If there are no breeders in your area, you can find legitimate and reliable breeders throughout the country on the national breed club lists. These established breeders can safely ship puppies to different states and even different countries. In order to avoid inadvertently purchasing from a puppy mill, always check the references of these breeders and do not hesitate to ask for documentation of their answers.

Puppy Mills

Puppy mills are large companies that breed mass quantities of purebred dogs. Dogs at these facilities are usually housed in small, overcrowded cages often piled several rows high. Because producing numerous puppies is the main objective, dogs are bred at every opportunity beginning when they have barely reached sexual maturity. In many cases dogs are born within just a year of their parents.

Temperament, one of the biggest concerns of reputable breeders, is also compromised in puppy mills. Lacking adequate human socialization, dogs often end up with an array of behavioral or emotional issues. Although these dogs usually come complete with American Kennel Club (AKC) paperwork, you will rarely be able to meet a dog's parents to get a feel for what the animal's temperament will likely be.

Since puppy mills have come under increased scrutiny in recent years, they have been forced to be more creative with their marketing techniques. Frequently, the puppies you see advertised for sale online or in your local newspaper are actually puppy mill dogs. The smoke and mirrors can be quite impressive, giving the appearance of a legitimate and caring operation. A telltale sign, though, is a common phone number for several different breeds. The only true way to

You can find reliable breeders through national breed clubs.

make sure you are buying from a responsible breeder is to visit the kennel personally.

Backyard Breeders

Some people will breed puppies purely for profit or out of ignorance. These are "backyard breeders," and many of the dogs they breed pass on genetic defects, may not find suitable homes, and end up in shelters. Watch for these signs of a backyard breeder:

- Breeds many litters per year.
- Knows little about the breed.
- Is not involved in the breed club or in dog sports.
- Claims not to know about or denies genetic problems in the breed or in the line.
- Has no health papers from the veterinarian.
- Will not let you see the whole litter, the place they were raised, or either of the puppies' parents.
- Does not socialize the dogs.
- Asks few or no questions about you or the environment in which the puppy will be raised.

SHELTERS

Most people do not put a lot of thought into acquiring a puppy. They fall in love with a cute face in a pet store window or with a neighborhood dog's new litter, or they get a dog from the kid selling puppies outside a supermarket. When the dog comes home, he may be too aggressive with the kids, too hard to housetrain, or hyperactive. They may complain that the puppy requires too much time and attention, sheds too much, barks and annoys the neighbors, destroys furniture, or displays a host of other problems. Often, too, someone may find that her unspayed female is pregnant and she either can't sell or take care of the puppies. Where do all of these dogs go?

Most of these dogs, through no fault of their own, end up in local humane societies and animal shelters throughout the country. Fortunately, these are sites where dedicated people work hard to place

Some people get a dog without understanding the breed's traits.

dogs in new homes and educate the public about responsible dog ownership. According to the Humane Society of the United States (HSUS), for every dog who has a home, there are nine other dogs who are homeless or in shelters.

Why do some animals end up in shelters? A study was recently conducted by the National Council on Pet Population whose researchers visited 12 animal shelters for one year and interviewed owners relinquishing their pets. The top ten reasons for giving up pets were as follows:

1. Moving
2. Landlord did not allow pet
3. Too many animals in household
4. Cost
5. Personal problems
6. Inadequate facilities

7. No homes available for littermates
8. No time to spend with pet
9. Illness
10. Biting

The study also found that about 47 percent of surrendered dogs were between five months and three years of age. Dogs acquired from friends were relinquished in higher numbers (31.4 percent) than from any other source, and about 95 percent had not received any obedience training.

Most animal shelters operate as independent agencies, although some fall under the jurisdiction of the city or county and operate with tax dollars. Humane societies are managed by their own board of directors and rely heavily on contributions and volunteers. Both share the common goal of finding homes for

> A purebred rescue group can be a good way to find a puppy.

as many dogs as possible, and most institutions will require spaying/neutering as a condition of adoption, offering special rates for these procedures.

Although you can visit your local animal shelters or humane societies during their regular hours, many also hold adoption days at pet supply stores and community events. If you find a dog you like, visit a few times and be sure to take the whole family. Ask as many questions as you can about the dog's background. Play with the pup away from the other dogs. In turn, the shelter will ask you about your dog-owning history and have you fill out a questionnaire that describes your home, work, and living situation and asks you to give veterinary references. This will help them make sure that the right dog goes to the right person.

Once you've been approved, you will pay an adoption fee. Some shelters will include vaccinations and training programs at a discounted rate. Although the actual adoption process will vary, people who adopt from shelters all go home with the same thing—a new best friend.

RESCUE

Most national breed clubs sponsor rescue groups that help place dogs into new homes. Although they mostly deal with adult dogs, a purebred rescue group can be a good way to find a puppy. Most of them work in conjunction with animal shelters, which alert the rescue organization if a purebred dog is brought in. The volunteers will provide foster homes for the dogs, assess their health and temperament, screen them for training and social skills, and care for the dogs until they find new homes.

As mentioned before, most of the dogs fostered in rescue programs are adults, but you can call and ask to be put on the waiting list for a puppy. You can get

in touch with a breed rescue in your area by calling the local humane society or the AKC. Both maintain a list of national breed rescue coordinators.

Most rescues deal with adults, but puppies are sometimes available.

4

SELECTING A HEALTHY PUPPY—FROM HEAD TO TOE

O nce you've decided on a breed and want to purchase or adopt a puppy, it's important to look at the big picture and clarify your expectations from your pet. Do you plan to become involved in the breeding or showing community? Do you have a preference for a male dog over female, or vice versa?

MALE VERSUS FEMALE

You'll get many different opinions about which sex you should choose. Some people swear that females are more easily trained and form closer emotional bonds with their owners. Others firmly believe that males have more character and more consistent temperaments.

Trust your breeder to find you the right puppy for your family.

When all is said and done, personality is subjective and varies from dog to dog. Gender is merely a matter of preference or even the luck of the draw. You may plan to view a litter of available puppies and lay claim to whichever puppy steals your heart…or chooses you!

Remember that, regardless of gender, you should alter (spay or neuter) your new puppy unless you plan to breed or show the dog in conformation. Not only will this prevent the birth of more unwanted puppies in an already overpopulated world, but there are advantages for the owner. By removing the sexual hormones and accompanying tensions, you will spare yourself the inconvenience of twice yearly estrus cycles ("heat") in females and the determined, more dominating nature of intact males. If you opt not to alter your pet dog, remember that you leave the female dog open to potential health issues such as false pregnancy and uterine cancer. Or your intact male may have a tendency to roam, requiring extra-vigilant supervision. When it comes to training the intact male, be ready to practice extra patience. Discuss the subject with your breeder or vet.

SHOW DOG VERSUS PET-QUALITY DOG

As you research breeders, you will no doubt discover that they may have varying prices for puppies of the same litter. Pups deemed show quality are more expensive than their pet-quality littermates, often with no discernible difference to the potential owner's eye. The lower price in no way represents an unhealthy or otherwise defective puppy;

Watching the litter and how they interact can tell you a lot about their general health as well as about the individual personalities of each puppy.

it simply indicates that the pet-quality pup will not grow into a dog suitable for conformation showing. He may have feet that turn out a wee bit more than the breed standard permits or a type of coloring that is unacceptable in the show ring. Physiological deviations from the breed standard don't portend future health problems, only that the dog doesn't sufficiently match the breed standard to make him a show contender.

A breeder will usually ask right away if you are interested in a family pet or a future champion. This will help her narrow your choices from the litter. A good breeder should guarantee the health of all her pups, regardless of conformation.

PICKING A HEALTHY PUP

When choosing a puppy, begin by examining the whole litter.

- In general, are they kept clean and sanitary?
- Are they handled regularly? The puppies should be kept in an environment that is conducive to socialization—they should be around people and handled regularly.
- Do the puppies look active and alert or do they look sluggish?
- Is the mother healthy looking and displaying a friendly temperament?
- Do the puppies seem fearful of people

How to Spot a Healthy Puppy

- Clear, bright eyes
- Pink, odor-free ears
- Clean, shiny coat
- Sweet "puppy" breath
- Clean anal region
- Alert, curious attitude

or are they inquisitive and curious?

Just watching the litter and how they interact can tell you a lot about their general health as well as about the individual personalities of each puppy.

Next, pick up and give each puppy a thorough once-over.

- A puppy should feel solid, with firm, well-developed muscles.
- A healthy puppy will not feel bony, bloated, or obese.
- Each puppy should have a clean and shiny coat, with no signs of irritation or sores on the skin.
- The eyes should be bright, clear, and free from discharge.
- Their ears should be pink inside and smell clean—a bad odor or waxy discharge could indicate ear mites.
- Their gums should be pink and their breath should smell sweet—not minty-fresh, but not sour or foul.
- Their anal region should be clean and dry, with no signs of diarrhea, discharge, or irritation.
- Obvious coughing, sneezing, or wheezing are clear indications of illness, as are runny eyes and noses.

Once you have determined that

Don't Do It!

Although it may be tempting to pick a sick puppy and take him home because you feel sorry for him, this is never a good idea. The heartache you will experience (and the veterinary bills) will not be worth it.

the puppies are healthy and you feel comfortable with the surroundings, you can begin to narrow down the choices in order to find the puppy who will best fit your needs, lifestyle, and personality.

TEMPERAMENT TESTING

Whether you have decided on a purebred or a mixed-breed puppy, the dog's temperament will be an important part of deciding which puppy you should take home. You will want to pick the puppy with a personality that will fit in with you and your family. You will also want to choose the puppy who will be able to do the things you want, whether it is to compete in events like obedience or agility, work as an assistance or therapy dog, or just take part in family activities. Not only are the dog's physical abilities important in this respect, but the puppy's temperament and trainability are large factors in picking the puppy you will be happy with (and that will be happy with you) for the rest of your lives together.

The Puppy Aptitude Test (PAT) is a method of evaluating a puppy's personality traits. Developed by renowned professional dog trainers Jack and Wendy Volhard, it has become the most widely used method for choosing a puppy. The method involves conducting a number of activities designed to evaluate confidence, dependence, dominance, and other personality traits, in addition to testing a puppy's structural soundness and sensitivities. It is a valuable tool in determining a puppy's suitability for various activities. The PAT evaluation can be found in its entirety on the Volhards' website at www.volhard.com.

If the final decision is up to you, watch the puppies play by themselves, with their dam and littermates, and with people. For most people, the pushiest puppy and the shyest puppy are not the best choices. A puppy who shows no interest in people may be more independent than you want. A prospective pet should be confident but not a bully, and he should be alert and interested in what's going on. Single encounters can fool you, though; if the puppies have played all afternoon, the one you think is calm and quiet may actually be a little fireball who just happens to be tired. That's why it's important to trust your breeder.

Trust Your Breeder

While temperament testing like the Volhard's method can be useful, your best tool for selecting a puppy is a good breeder who watches and interacts extensively with her puppies for weeks and who listens to what you want and don't want in a dog. She can choose or help you choose the right pup based on much more information than you can get in one or two short visits.

A breeder will usually ask right away if you are interested in a family pet or a show dog.

Observe the Parents

When choosing a puppy, you should be able to see and observe the temperament and behavior of both the dam and littermates. A puppy will often display the characteristics and personality of the parents.

Allow the breeder to help you select the right dog. She's been observing you while you have been observing the puppy. At this point, she should know about you, your family, your lifestyle, and your goals, and she probably has an idea of what pup will work best in your home. It helps if you know your own mind as well. Are you looking for a pet, a hunt prospect, or a show dog? Are you interested in obedience, agility, or just wandering around the dog park? Be as honest as possible, and you'll end up with a better dog for your home.

By now, you have done your research, decided on and found the type of puppy you want, confirmed the pup's health, and tested temperament. You have done all you can to ensure that you get off to a good start, even before you bring your new puppy home. The big day is here! Now it's time to prepare for your new addition!

5

GETTING
PREPARED

There are a few things you should do before a puppy steps into your home. To ensure that you begin on the right foot, remember that puppies are just like babies. You wouldn't bring home a new baby before you had a crib, diapers, clothes, and all of the other equipment you need to keep a child safe and comfortable. The same holds true for your new canine addition.

VETERINARY CARE

The first thing you should do is find a good veterinarian in your area. Within 72 hours of arriving home, your pup should visit the vet for a complete exam and to continue a vaccination schedule. Also, you never know when an emergency may arise, so select your veterinarian before bringing your puppy home.

Choosing your pup's "personal physician" takes time and research. The vet will be one of the most important people in your puppy's life, so choose carefully. The best way to find a good vet is to ask around among your friends and neighbors and see where they go and why they like that particular veterinarian. What do they like about that clinic? Is it one vet they like, or do they like everyone at the clinic? Do they have strong preferences about which vet to see? Also, ask any local veterinary associations, dog clubs, dog schools, or dog groups for recommendations.

From these recommendations, cull through the list by determining location and hours. If an emergency occurs, the closer you are, the better. That is not to say you should choose based on location, but if you come down to two perfectly good choices, location may make a difference.

Visit the top two clinics on your list and see how the staff interacts with both animals and clients. Tell them on the phone that you are shopping for a new vet. You can get a gut feeling by standing in the lobby and seeing the staff interact with clients. Don't be afraid to ask for an appointment to tour the facility.

Find a veterinarian before you bring your puppy home.

Pricing

Because clinics have different approaches to pricing, comparing clinics on price alone is like comparing apples to oranges. One clinic may have a higher fee for a dental cleaning because they use better anesthesia and monitoring equipment, so don't choose based on price alone. Low prices may mean a lower standard of care with which you may not be comfortable, or it may mean you end up with a lot of extra fees incurred to make up for a low price designed to get you in the door. It might also mean your vet went to vet school a long time ago, no longer needs to pay back school loans, and is a perfectly fine vet. Just don't let price be your only consideration.

Services

Find out what services are available. Do they have a groomer on staff, or do they board dogs? Is anyone there overnight? Do they have any specialists on staff? Do they have a network of specialists with whom they work on a regular basis?

How does the clinic handle after-hours emergencies, and what do clients do for urgent care? Dogs are notorious for getting sick in the middle of the night or on holidays—will you have to go to an emergency hospital, or will the staff meet you at their clinic? How far away is the emergency hospital they recommend?

Quality of Care

Ask if each dog has a full physical exam prior to every surgery. This added precaution may uncover a previously

Your puppy's vet will be one of the most important people in his life.

undetected concern. How early can you drop off your dog for surgery? How late can you pick him up? Ask what safety precautions are taken during surgery—do they put breathing tubes on all anesthetized patients? Do they have a heart and oxygen monitor? Do they have a crash box for cardiac emergencies? Is a fresh sterilized surgical pack used for each surgery?

Ask what safety precautions are taken after surgery. A dog's temperature should be monitored in case he gets too cold, which can negatively affect his heart.

Another significant factor is how they manage pain for their patients. Veterinarians who stay current know how to manage pain; the difference between pain management today and even a decade ago is astounding. Some surgeries, such as orthopedic surgery, are more painful to recuperate from than others, and the ease with which your dog recuperates on appropriate pain control is significant. If a veterinarian tells you that animals don't feel pain the way humans do, keep looking. No reason exists for your dog to be in pain after surgery.

You want to establish a good working relationship with someone you trust. You may be seeing a lot of the clinic, so make sure you're comfortable with it. I see my veterinarian far, far more frequently than I see my own physician. If you're interested in alternative medicine or feeding a raw diet, ask how they feel about this to see if they think it's ineffective or a valuable option. It's best to work with someone who shares your philosophies. Most people choose a veterinarian based on how they feel about the person: It's the personal touch that matters.

LICENSE TO OWN

Make sure your pooch is legal. Call your town hall or animal control office and ask when your dog requires a license, which is usually at about six months of age. Many towns will also require proof that your dog has been vaccinated for rabies. Find out what other local laws apply to your dog. Most towns have leash laws and clean-up laws, with stiff fines for people who don't follow them. You should

Naming a new puppy may be one of the most enjoyable aspects of getting one.

also get your dog an ID tag that states the dog's name and your name, address, and phone number. This will be very helpful in case the dog gets lost.

WHAT'S IN A NAME?

Naming a new puppy may be one of the most enjoyable aspects of getting one. Some people like to pick a name that indicates the dog's origins or appearance, (I know an Australian Shepherd named Sydney and an Irish Setter named Copper) or their other interests. (I know a Star Trek fan who has a Beagle named Spock and an English professor who has two chocolate Labs named Romeo and Juliet.) Some people choose "people" names like Fred, Chester, Rosie, or Jake. Names can come from anywhere: cities, television

that your puppy will need immediately, so it is best to purchase these items before he comes home. The better prepared you are for the puppy's arrival, the smoother the transition will be for everyone.

Baby Gates

Baby gates are very useful for keeping your puppy confined in a safe place. You can also block the puppy's access to other rooms and stairs, or restrict access to anything that may be unsafe.

Bed

Beds come in all shapes, colors, sizes, and materials. Choose a size that will fit your puppy comfortably. Before you spend a lot of money on a quality bed, you may want to wait until your puppy is past his chewing stage, at around nine months. Otherwise, you may discover that he thinks the beautiful bed you bought him to nap on is much better for chewing! There are some chew-resistant beds on the market if you have a real power chewer. You also can spray the bed with chew-deterrent spray. If your puppy insists on shredding his bed or crate pad, however, it's best to remove it altogether rather than risk him eating it and getting a stomach obstruction.

Collar and Leash

One of the first things your puppy should learn is to wear a collar and walk on a leash. You should buy an adjustable, soft, nylon buckle collar. The collar should fit snugly against your puppy's neck. When you slip your fingers in between the collar and his neck, you should only be able

shows, literature, movies—all it takes is a little imagination to pick a name that perfectly fits your puppy's personality.

You should try to make the puppy's name short, one or two syllables, and you shouldn't pick a name that may sound too close to a command, like Six or Downy, which may confuse your dog during training. Most of all, you should never say your puppy's name in a loud or threatening tone or call the dog to you for a scolding. You want your puppy to jump with joy and excitement when hearing his name, no matter what it is!

SUPPLIES FOR YOUR PUPPY

Shopping for your puppy can be fun! While you might not need everything on this list right away, there are certain things to get two flat fingers underneath the collar. You may worry that the collar is too tight, but having too loose a collar is dangerous. He could slip loose, or if his jaw becomes caught in the collar, he could panic and hurt himself.

Avoid choke chains, prong collars, or slip collars for your puppy. These can cause damage to his throat, and they are not necessary when you use modern, reward-based training methods.

Always remove your puppy's collar when he's in his crate. The collar or tags on the collar could get caught in the door or wire frame of the crate and cause him to choke.

Get your puppy a 4- to 6-foot (1- to 2-m) cotton, nylon, or leather leash. Don't use a retractable leash to train your puppy.

They're bulky to hold when training, and they always keep tension on your puppy's collar. If he gets used to this sensation, he may learn to pull when he's on a regular leash to keep that same tension. After your puppy has learned not to pull on leash, a retractable leash may not be so confusing. They are good for exercising your puppy, especially if you don't have a fenced yard.

Crate

A crate serves as a dog's own room. It is a very important purchase because it has so many uses: It is a great housetraining tool, a safe way for your dog to travel, and a comfortable bed where the pup can sleep, retreat, and relax. Using a crate is the easiest and fastest way to housetrain

Choose a bed size that will fit your puppy comfortably.

COMPLETE GUIDE TO PUPPY CARE

A soft, adjustable nylon collar and leash are essential items for your puppy.

and is great when you can't supervise your dog.

The two most common types of crates are plastic or fiberglass airline-type crates with enclosed sides and open metal wire crates. The plastic crates are good to use for traveling, especially by air, and some dogs feel more secure in an enclosed space. The wire crates provide more ventilation in hotter weather and more room to move around. Consider how you will be using the crate and pick the best one to fit your needs.

A crate is an expensive item, so buy one that will fit your dog's adult size. An adult dog should be able to stand up, turn around, and stretch out in the crate. However, you don't want your little puppy to have too much room either. Some crates come with a divider that lets you expand the crate as the puppy grows.

Or you can block the back of the crate with a piece of plywood when the pup is small and make the space bigger as he matures.

Exercise Pen (Ex-Pen)

An exercise pen is an enclosure made up of panels that fold up for travel or storage purposes. It is open at the top and bottom. Depending on the size and number of panels, exercise pens can be small or quite roomy.

If you travel with your puppy, an exercise pen is a real convenience. You can set it up and give your puppy a small, "fenced-in yard" to stretch his legs. It also can be a good transition from a crate— rather than giving your puppy the run of an entire room, you can see how he does with the greater freedom of an exercise pen first.

Ten Essential Items for Your Puppy

1. Baby gates
2. Collar
3. Crate
4. Food bowl
5. Grooming tools
6. ID Tag
7. Leash
8. Puppy food
9. Toys
10. Water bowl

Food and Water Bowls

When it comes to food and water bowls for your puppy, there is one guarantee—chewable bowls will be chewed and breakable bowls will be broken. Nothing could be more fun for your puppy than spilling food and water all over your kitchen floor. The best bowls to buy are stainless steel or ceramic bowls that are wide on the bottom and heavy so that they won't spill, saving you hours of cleanup and lots of money in the long run.

Grooming Tools

No matter what breed, your puppy will need to be groomed on a regular basis. You will need to purchase some basic grooming tools such as a comb and brush (the type of comb and brush you buy will depend on the kind of coat your puppy has), nail clippers, and a good dog shampoo and conditioner.

Halters and Harnesses

If your puppy really pulls hard on the leash, if he jumps on people a lot, or if he's a large, strong puppy and you're having difficulty walking him, you may find a head halter or harness helpful.

Canine head halters operate on the same principle as head halters for horses. A nose loop on the halter gives you greater control over your puppy's head. Control the head, control the puppy. Head halters are not muzzles. Your puppy can still eat, give kisses, and drink while wearing a head halter.

Several different brands are available. Be sure that the person who sells you a head halter knows how to properly fit it. Your puppy may need some time to get used to having a loop over his nose. You can speed this along by offering him treats through the nose loop.

A head halter may help control a puppy who pulls hard on the leash.

Harnesses are another popular option. If you have a flat-faced breed of dog such as a Pug or Bulldog who has difficulty breathing in certain situations, a harness may be a better option than a regular collar because it doesn't go across your puppy's throat. A harness that has a hook in the back for a leash will not stop your dog from pulling. Think about what they hook Huskies up to sleds with—harnesses! Harnesses redistribute a dog's weight across the back and chest so that your puppy will actually pull more efficiently. If he has an issue with pulling on the leash, try one of the newer harnesses that feature a leash hook in front. These seem to teach puppies better "body sense" so that they don't pull as much as they do with regular harnesses.

Identification

Every dog should have an identification tag attached to his collar that has his owner's name, address, and phone number engraved on it. This information will make it easier for someone to contact you in the event that your puppy should become lost.

There are several methods of dog identification available today. The first is tattooing. The dog's inner thigh or ear flap is permanently tattooed with numbers that are then registered with one of the national registries. This makes it possible for the registry companies to contact you if your dog turns up at a shelter. Also, research laboratories will not take dogs who have been tattooed.

Second is the microchip, a small computer chip that can be placed under your dog's skin. If a dog is picked up by animal control, the chip can be scanned and the dog's owner can be identified. There are a few microchip registry companies in practice, and they do share information with each other.

Puppy Food

Speak to your breeder and find out what the puppy has been eating. It is wise to

purchase the same food for at least the first few weeks. Switching food suddenly can cause stomach upset and diarrhea. If you wish to change the brand of food, you can do so gradually over an extended period of time. The feeding chapter will give you more details on the best nutrition for your puppy.

Toys and Chews

All puppies need to chew as part of their physical and mental development. At about four weeks of age, your puppy's deciduous (baby) teeth will come in. Pups will need to strengthen their jaw muscles and make room for future adult teeth. Chewing helps them to explore the world. Good, safe toys will entertain and give your puppy something to chew on other than your shoes or furniture. Not only are toys healthy, they are a fun way of keeping your puppy occupied. Playing together will help to strengthen the bond between the two of you.

SETTLING IN

Once you have all the basic equipment ready for your puppy, you should set up a tentative schedule with your family. Figure out who can be with the pup and

when because any dog needs constant supervision for the first few days. The worst thing you can do is to leave a new puppy alone. He will be unsure of the environment. Your puppy will be scared and lonely, and his first impressions will last a long time.

Think about where the puppy will eat, sleep, and be taken to eliminate. It is also a good time to take a look at your existing environment and see if your home is safe enough for the pup.

PUPPY-PROOFING YOUR HOME

Your new puppy will be very curious about his new surroundings, and with typical puppy energy, will want to investigate everything. The trick is to make the dangerous things unavailable by puppy-proofing your home. The best way to do this is to get down on the pup's level and take a look around. What can he get into? What can he jump up on? What can your pup open or chew on? Don't ever assume that the puppy won't touch something; if pups can get into trouble, they will. There are many potential dangers in the home, so you must think about these in advance and make sure your new puppy is protected from them.

Balconies

If you live in an apartment building or house that has a balcony, you must make sure that your puppy cannot fall. Check the railings on your patio, balcony, or deck, and if the space between them is too large, you can use inexpensive chicken wire or baby gates to form a temporary screen.

Bathrooms

When puppy-proofing your home, bathrooms should be treated like kitchens. Securely fasten or lock all cupboards and medicine chests.

Keep all cleansers and detergents out of reach. Place all soaps and shampoos in a shower caddy so that your puppy can't get to them. Be especially careful of decorative soaps—if they smell good, your puppy will try to eat them.

Keep the toilet seat cover down at all times. Curious puppies have been known to climb up and fall in. The best advice is to keep doors shut to all rooms where the puppy should not have access unless you can supervise him. Puppies can't get into trouble if they can't get to the trouble in the first place.

Make sure your puppy has safe toys to chew on.

Electrical Wires

Be sure that all electrical wires are hidden from view and not plugged in when not in use. Even wires from appliances that are turned off, such as lamps or television sets, can be dangerous. To be safe, unplug anything electric if it is not currently being used.

Garage

If you have a garage or tool shed, make sure that this is puppy-proofed too. Many people keep potential hazards to their pets in garages, such as antifreeze, motor oil, gasoline, fertilizer, insecticides, paint, and paint removers, among other things. People also keep tools in the garage, such as saws, hammers, nails, and knives, which obviously can be very dangerous as well. Put these things out of your puppy's reach or keep them safely locked up.

Your puppy will be scared and lonely the first few days, so set up a schedule so that he's constantly supervised.

Kitchen

Your puppy will probably spend a lot of time in the kitchen. It is usually where most of the family congregates and is probably the most convenient place to feed your pup and to clean up any messes he may make.

However, the kitchen can be filled with lots of dangers. Make sure the cupboards are securely fastened at all times or buy locks. Place all cleaning supplies, detergents, and solvents in locked cupboards, or place them well out of your dog's reach.

It is also a good idea to keep the garbage hidden or the lid tightly closed. There is nothing more tempting to dogs than the aroma of garbage, and nothing could be worse for them. The garbage may hold spoiled food or items like chicken bones or chocolate, which can make them seriously ill.

Be careful of what you are leaving on tables or counters as well. Everyone has heard the story of the dog who jumped up and ate the Thanksgiving turkey, the Easter candy, or the birthday cake left on the counter. It may not seem as if your tiny pup can get up that high, but puppies are ingenious at getting into things they shouldn't—especially if it involves food.

Also, be careful when cooking. Rambunctious puppies can jump up and knock over pots and pans, causing serious injury. It is a good idea to confine your puppy to a crate before you cook a meal.

Open Doors

Puppies can easily get underfoot or sneak up on you. A door may seem like a pretty harmless object, but if it is slammed shut, either by a draft or by accident, it could easily kill or injure a puppy. During warm weather, windows or doors are left open and people are more likely to

Laundry Hints

More than one puppy has climbed into the washing machine for a quick nap and been caught in the rinse cycle instead. If the washing machine door is open, be sure to check inside the machine before you close the door and switch the machine on.

run in and out. Know where your puppy is at all times and make sure that everyone in your household knows to keep doors securely shut.

Ponds and Pools

Lots of dogs like the water and love to swim, but your puppy must be taught to get in and out of your pool safely. Many dogs will jump headfirst into a swimming pool and have no idea how to get out. There will

Some dogs love water—even from their drinking bowl!

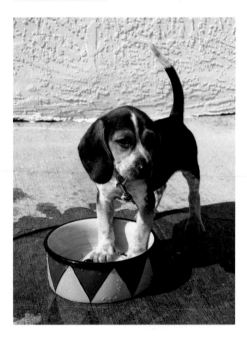

be plenty of time to introduce swimming as the puppy strengthens and matures. Never leave your puppy unsupervised near water, and keep pools or ponds covered if you can't be there. It only takes a few minutes for a puppy to drown while your back is turned.

Yard

The yard should be a fun place for your puppy to hang out and play, but you must take the necessary precautions to make it as safe as possible. First, you must make sure that the yard is securely fenced and that there is no way for your puppy to escape. Check that all fences are strong and that there are no holes in the wire or near the ground. Make sure

that there is a secure lock on the gate and that everyone in your family knows to fasten it when they come in or out of the yard. Pick up any toys, lawn furniture, or gardening tools that you don't want your puppy to play with. Whatever puppies can chew, they will.

If there is a particular area of your yard where you do not want your puppy to go, such as the garden, fence that area off. Be careful what pesticides or fertilizers you use on your lawn. Do not let the puppy into a yard where chemicals have been used. Make sure you store any chemicals where your puppy can't get to them.

Remember that some plants are poisonous to puppies. Check your yard to

You must take the necessary precautions to make your yard as safe as possible for your puppy.

Plants That Are Poisonous to Your Dog

amaryllis bulb	elderberry	monkshood
andromeda	elephant ear	mushrooms
apple seeds	English ivy	narcissus
arrowgrass	foxglove	nightshade
azalea	hemlock	oleander
bittersweet	holly	peach
boxwood	hyacinth	philodendron
buttercup	hydrangea	poison ivy
caladium	iris	privet
castor bean	Japanese yew	rhododendron
cherry pits	jasmine berries	rhubarb
chokecherry	Jerusalem cherry	snow on the mountain
climbing lily	jimson weed	stinging nettle
crown of thorns	laburnum	toadstool
daffodil bulb	larkspur	tobacco
daphne	laurel	tulip bulb
delphinium	marigold	walnut
dieffenbachia	marijuana	wisteria
dumb cane	mistletoe berries	yew

make sure these plants are not present. If your dog eats something he shouldn't, you can call the National Animal Poison Control Center (NAPCC) at 1-800-548-2423.

They have a staff of over 40 licensed vets and board certified toxicologists. They can be reached 24 hours a day.

If your fence is not secure or you don't want to give your puppy free rein of the yard, you may want to consider building a dog run. It should be about 20 feet (6 m) long and about 6 feet (2 m) wide and should have some shade. You should also provide water and a clean, comfortable place for the pup to lie down.

PREPARING THE KIDS

When you are ready to bring your puppy home, it is very likely that the most excited members of your family will be your children. However, in their enthusiasm, children can get carried away and unintentionally hurt or frighten a small puppy. To make sure that the transition goes as smoothly as possible, you must set some ground rules before the puppy arrives.

Children should be taught from the outset that a puppy is not a plaything to be dragged around, and they should be scolded promptly if they disobey. Toddlers and small children should never

be left unsupervised with puppies. They must be taught to respect animals and to be gentle with them. If the puppy is frightened by children, the feeling might continue as the pup matures. Also, the puppy may nip or scratch in fear, which could harm or scare your children. Mutual regard for one another must be taught from the outset. Teach children that your puppy is a living thing with feelings and can be hurt. Make sure that the pup is given a break and allowed to have quiet time away from excited "siblings."

Children also must be shown how to lift a puppy safely. Teach your kids to place the right hand under the pup's chest, then use the left hand to hold the pup's neck.

Children should be taught to respect puppies.

Now they can lift the dog and bring him close to their chest, supporting the rump with their left hand. Never lift a pup by the ears or by the scruff of the neck.

Remember that puppies are very much like children. Most likely, the puppy will find your child to be the most exciting person in the house. But puppies, much like children, need limits. They also need to rest often and be allowed to relax. If you teach your puppy and your child to be gentle and respect each other, there is no doubt that they will soon become the best of friends.

A Child's Ten Commandments for Puppy Care

Go over the following "commandments" with your child. Print them out and post them on the fridge to remind the kids how to properly interact with the puppy.

1. Thou shall treat all animals as you would like to be treated—gently, kindly, and respectfully.
2. Thou shall not lift the puppy unless you have been taught to do it properly and an adult is nearby.
3. Thou shall not disturb the puppy while he is eating or sleeping.
4. Thou shall not share your snacks.
5. Thou shall keep your toys and the puppy's toys separate.
6. Thou shall not tease.
7. Thou shall not approach any strange dog.
8. Thou shall help the puppy follow the rules of the house and not allow him to disobey the rules.
9. Thou shall honor your puppy as a living thing and take responsibility for his care and well-being.
10. Thou shall enjoy the years of love and friendship your puppy gives you—and remember to give it back.

6

PUPPY
COMES HOME

You've been shopping, your house is ready, your kids are ready, you are ready—it's time to pick up your puppy. If possible, you should arrange to take a few days off. If this is not possible, pick up the puppy on a Friday in order to spend as much time as you can helping him get adjusted. A morning pickup is best because that will give the puppy all day to explore his new surroundings.

If the breeder is only a short distance away, you should bring a small cardboard box or a crate for the pup, a blanket, and towels to clean up any messes. Puppies tend to get carsick, especially if it is their first ride, and they may throw up or urinate. Keeping the car well ventilated may help. Also, be sure to tell the breeder what time you will be picking the puppy up so that the dog's meals can be planned accordingly.

If it is a longer ride, make frequent stops. Bring along a collar and leash so you can take the dog out to exercise and potty. Do not let your new pup near other dogs or where other dogs have been until all vaccinations have been completed.

LEAVING THE BREEDER

Before you leave the breeder, there are certain documents you should receive that will include important information about your puppy.

Inoculation Record

The breeder should have initiated the necessary inoculations by the time the puppies are eight weeks of age, so your puppy should have been given his first shots before leaving the breeder. These inoculations protect the puppies against hepatitis, leptospirosis, distemper, and canine parvovirus. In most cases, rabies inoculations are not given until a puppy is four months of age or older. (A suggested schedule for inoculations is given in the health chapter.)

Inoculations are usually given as a series, and it is very important that your puppy receives the full set in order for them to be effective. Be sure that the breeder provides you with the puppy's record and the name of her veterinarian before you bring your pup home. This way, you can show the information to

Leaving the Nest

The best time for a puppy to leave his mother is generally about nine weeks of age. Before the seventh week, puppies are not mentally mature or independent enough to leave the security of their mom and littermates. At eight weeks, puppies go through a fear-imprinting period. Any experience that frightens a puppy at this stage, such as an unpleasant car ride or rough play with children, may remain with him for a long time. If you do bring home a puppy in the eighth week, make sure that you provide him with many positive experiences.

the veterinarian you have chosen, who will then be able to continue with an appropriate inoculation schedule.

Pedigree

If your puppy is a purebred, the breeder must supply you with a pedigree. This shows your puppy's ancestors back to at least the third generation. The pedigree can be helpful in determining if your puppy's relatives have titles in conformation, agility, obedience, or field trials, which can indicate the trainability and work ethic of the pup's parents, grandparents, etc.

Registration Certificate

A national kennel club registry issues a registration certificate when the puppy's

Before you leave the breeder's you should have all of your puppy's paperwork in order.

parents and ancestors are also registered. When ownership of a puppy is transferred from the breeder's name to your name, the transfer is recorded on this document. Once this is mailed to the kennel club, it is permanently recorded in their files.

Diet Sheet

Most breeders will give the new owner a written record detailing the amount and kind of food a puppy has been eating. Follow these recommendations exactly, at least for the first few weeks after the puppy comes to live with you.

The instructions should indicate the number of times a day your puppy has been fed, as well as the kind of vitamin supplementation, if any. If you follow the breeder's instructions, it will greatly reduce the chance of your puppy suffering from an upset stomach and diarrhea.

The breeder's diet sheet should project the food increases and changes that will be necessary as your puppy grows. If the breeder does not provide you with this information, ask your veterinarian for suggestions. If and when you decide to change the type or brand of dog food you are giving your puppy, do so gradually, mixing the old food with the new until the substitution is completed.

Health Guarantee

Reputable breeders will be more than willing to supply a written agreement that the puppy you take home must be able to pass a veterinarian's examination. Furthermore, they should offer a guarantee against the development of any hereditary problems. As mentioned before, you should arrange an appointment with a veterinarian within a few days of bringing the pup home. Most breeders are as anxious as you to ensure that the puppy is happy and comfortable in your home. Many will give you a breed book that has instructions on basic care and training. Breeders want to follow the progress of their dogs, so they will be willing to answer any questions you may have.

Adoption Paperwork

If you are taking your puppy home from a humane society or animal shelter,

you will not get all the paperwork that you will get from a breeder. Depending on the organization, you will probably leave with an inoculation record and a feeding schedule that includes the brand of dog food used at the shelter. You may also get information on training classes available in the area. If you have any questions about the dog's health or care, ask. Most shelter volunteers are eager to help you make your puppy as comfortable as possible.

THE FIRST FEW DAYS

The first few nights that a puppy spends away from mom and littermates may be frightening. Being in a strange environment with new sounds and new people will probably make your pup feel scared, insecure, and lonely. It is

Let your puppy explore his new surroundings at his own pace.

uncertain when he gets to play with you will be forever begging you to play a game. This doesn't mean that you can't ever forget the routine or give him extra attention; it does mean, though, that he should expect certain things at certain times. Although it may seem like a chore to develop a fixed routine for your puppy, in the long run it will make life a lot easier for both of you.

Your new puppy should learn the following things about your house within the first few days:

- Where his food and water dishes are
- When he gets fed
- Where his crate or bed is located
- When he gets to go out
- When people get up and go to bed
- Where his toys are

Knowing these things will help make him comfortable and confident. Dogs whose schedules are switched, food bowls moved around, and who are subjected to varying times for walks have more trouble housetraining and just figuring out their place in the world.

very important to try to make your new addition as comfortable as possible, which is why it's a good idea to take some time off to help with the transition. Try to refrain from overwhelming the dog with new people or things, and allow him to adjust and to explore your home at his own pace. Introduce the schedule that you have set up to establish a routine as soon as possible.

The Schedule

Puppies really rely on regular routines and structure to build their confidence and give them a sense of security. A puppy who never knows when he's going to be fed next will be constantly whining for dinner. A puppy who never knows when walk time is will demand to go out all the time. A puppy who is

It's All in the Papers

All purebred dogs have a pedigree. The pedigree does not imply that a dog is show quality–it is simply a chronological list of ancestors. Also, registration papers only guarantee that a dog is registerable, nothing else. Neither paper is a guarantee of the health nor quality of your dog.

First Night

Trainer Alexandra Allred has a tip to help your puppy adjust to his new home: Allow the pup to sleep with a few articles of your clothing, preferably something you have worn that smells like you. This way, your puppy will become adjusted to your scent and will feel more comfortable in this new environment.

Nighttime

Your puppy may whimper or cry at night. For the first few nights, you should provide as much comfort as possible by offering a warm blanket, soft toys, and a dim night light. However, don't let the pup do anything now that you are not planning to allow in the future. For example, if you do not want your dog to sleep on the bed or the furniture, don't allow him to do so now. However, you might bring your pup's bed or crate into your room to be near you. As the days pass, the youngster will become used to the new environment and should become more comfortable.

The worst thing you can do is yell at or scold a scared puppy for making noise or crying. This will only make matters worse and teach your puppy to fear you instead of trust you. Remember that each puppy is an individual and will need different levels of attention. It is important to find a balance between coddling and comforting.

Other Pets

If you have other pets in your home, you will need to introduce the puppy to them carefully, depending on what kind

Make sure your pup has a warm blanket to snuggle in at night.

of pets you already have. Puppies will usually have no problems meeting other animals, but the other animal whose turf is being invaded may have a problem with the puppy. The best thing to do is to keep them separated until they are used to each other. Most older dogs will accept a puppy without a fuss and will quickly teach the puppy who is the boss. Cats will not have a lot of patience with a rambunctious, playful puppy, and he may get a scratch for stepping over the line. Also, small animals like rabbits or hamsters should be kept out of the puppy's reach. If you make introductions

Most older dogs will accept a new puppy, but you should still carefully supervise introductions.

slowly and carefully and supervise the animals when they are together, they will eventually learn to coexist and may even become good friends in the process.

Now your puppy is safe and sound and may even be starting to like his new home. However, your journey is just beginning. Remember that you are responsible for all of the aspects of this youngster's care—mental and physical. Part Two will show you how to keep your puppy physically healthy.

Quarantine!
Dogs can transmit diseases to other dogs, and people can carry bacteria on their hands or clothes that can be passed to the puppy. Until vaccinations have been completed, it is best to limit visitors, both canine and human.

PART TWO
CARING FOR
YOUR PUPPY

7

HEALTH CARE

There are few things sadder than a sick puppy. Luckily, you can ensure your puppy's good health by being a responsible owner and providing everything needed to maintain his well-being. Your puppy cannot take himself to the veterinarian, set up a vaccination schedule, check for parasites, or handle an emergency. This is all up to you. The better care you take of your puppy now, the longer you'll have a wonderful companion. Remember, a healthy puppy is a happy puppy!

HOW TO RECOGNIZE A HEALTHY PUPPY

Your puppy should be the picture of good health and appear vibrant, alert, and interested in the world. Check your pup's body on a regular basis. If you know how things look when they are normal, it will be easier for you to detect any abnormalities that might occur.

Health Check

A healthy puppy or dog should display these characteristics:

- **Eyes**—Bright, clear, and free of redness, discharge, or inflammation
- **Nose**—Moist, not dry or cracked, and free of discharge
- **Ears**—Should look clean and smell pleasant with no soreness or redness
- **Mouth**—Fresh breath and firm, pink gums with no redness or bleeding; no broken or missing teeth
- **Body**—No indication of pain or

At the first visit, the veterinarian will check your puppy's overall health.

Life Span According to Size

Your puppy will be around for many years, depending on his size, breed, health care, and breeding. There is an average life span for each size and breed, so make every year of your puppy's life a healthy one!

DOG SIZE	TYPICAL LIFE SPAN	BREEDS INCLUDE
Small: up to 20 lbs (9 kg)	15 years	Miniature and Toy Poodles, Pomeranians, Shih Tzu, Yorkshire Terriers, etc.
Medium: 20 to 50 lbs (9 to 23 kg)	11 to 13 years	Australian Shepherds, Cocker Spaniels, English Springer Spaniels, Keeshonden, etc.
Large: 50 to 80 lbs (23 to 36 kg)	8 to 10 years	German Shepherd Dogs, Golden Retrievers, Labrador Retrievers, Rottweilers, etc.
Giant: over 80 lbs (36 kg)	9 years	Great Danes, Great Pyrenees, Newfoundlands, Saint Bernards, etc.

tenderness; no lumps, bumps, or red spots

- **Anal area**—Clean and free of any debris; anal sacs on either side of the anus should not be swollen
- **Coat**—Free from mats and any other debris, like flea dirt (little black specks); skin should not appear dry or flaky
- **Legs**—No pain or stiffness
- **Feet**—No lumps, sores, burrs, or any other foreign objects; pads should be examined for cuts and nails checked for length

If you perform an all-over exam on a daily basis, it will be easy to spot any problems before they become serious.

VETERINARY CARE

In this section, we will discuss your pup's basic veterinary requirements in more detail. As we discussed in Chapter 5, select a veterinarian before you need one. Finding one during an emergency isn't a good start, and your stress will be significantly less if you have an established relationship with a veterinarian.

Statistics show that two out of three pets will experience major medical problems in the course of their lifetime. The high cost of some veterinary procedures, which can run into thousands of dollars, has forced owners who may not have the money into making tough choices, watching their pets suffer, or euthanizing them. To help defray expenses, more and more owners are turning to pet insurance. There are several companies that offer this type of insurance.

THE FIRST CHECKUP

You will want to take your new puppy for a first checkup within 48 to 72 hours after bringing him home. A puppy can appear healthy at first but may have a serious problem that is not immediately apparent. Many pets have some minor condition that may never become a real problem. Unfortunately, if the dog does have a serious problem, you may want to consider returning the pet, especially if you have children—attachments will be formed that may have to be broken prematurely.

At the first visit, the veterinarian will check your puppy's overall health, which includes listening to the heart; checking the respiration; feeling the abdomen, muscles, and joints; checking the mouth, including the gum color and signs of gum disease, as well as plaque buildup; checking the ears for signs of an infection or ear mites; examining the eyes; and last but not least, checking the condition of the skin and coat.

Next, your vet will discuss the proper diet and the quantity of food to give your puppy. If this is different from your breeder's recommendation, then

Your vet will discuss the proper diet for your puppy.

you should discuss those suggestions with your vet as well. If you decide to change the diet, it should be done over a prolonged period of time so as not to cause gastrointestinal upset.

It is also customary to take a small stool sample to test for intestinal parasites. It must be fresh, preferably within the last 12 hours, because the eggs hatch quickly and may not be observed under the microscope. If your puppy won't oblige, the technician can usually take one in the clinic.

VACCINATIONS

Vaccines can prevent diseases that can cause your puppy to become seriously ill. Canine distemper used to rage through kennels, shelters, and neighborhoods,

Ask your veterinarian about your puppy's recommended vaccination protocol.

and parvo killed countless puppies and adult dogs. If you purchase a puppy from a responsible source and then correctly vaccinate your dog, you will not have to worry about these diseases.

The old advice used to be that your dog needed vaccinations against several diseases as a puppy and that your adult dog should get booster shots every year. The old thinking was that a vaccine wasn't going to hurt anything, and it was better to vaccinate for everything (and repeat the vaccinations every year) than to risk the health of a dog. Then, veterinarians started noticing some problems in cats. In 1998, concerns about increased rates of a certain kind of cancer in cats at vaccine-injection sites were reported in the *Journal of the American Veterinary Medical Association*. Subsequent studies have demonstrated that between 1 in 1,000 and 1 in 10,000 cats will develop cancer from receiving vaccines.

Those discoveries in cats underscored the fact that vaccines aren't entirely harmless. They are powerful agents going into your dog's body. While dogs don't seem to have vaccine-related cancers, some reports suggest that certain kinds of health problems, such as allergies, may be exacerbated by overvaccinating.

Today's pet lovers look for a happy medium: ensuring that their dogs are well protected but not overvaccinated. Frankly, where to draw that line is still being studied by the veterinary community. The problem is that, as of now, no one knows for sure how long a vaccine provides immunity. Currently, studies are underway to determine how long a vaccination will protect your dog against disease, so in the future, recommended vaccine protocols may change.

The following is being recommended by most veterinary schools throughout the country at this time.

Core Vaccines

No controversy surrounds the basics: All puppies need core immunizations against the most deadly diseases. A puppy's mother's milk gives him immunity for the first several weeks of his life (assuming she is healthy and was given the proper vaccinations). After your puppy is weaned, vaccinations give him his own immunity.

Puppy vaccines are given in a series between the ages of about six weeks and four months. Although many people assume that these shots gradually build up a puppy's immunity, this is not the case. A puppy who still has temporary immunity from his mother's milk won't receive immunity from a vaccination. The problem is that it is impossible to know exactly when the mother's temporary immunity will wear off, so the puppy vaccines are repeated until the age of four months.

Every puppy should have these core vaccinations: rabies, parvovirus, distemper, and adenovirus-2 (which also protects against canine infectious hepatitis). These diseases are still widespread, and they can be deadly if the animal comes down with them. Vaccines for these diseases have a low likelihood of side effects.

Non-Core Vaccines

Other diseases are less widespread, and whether a vaccine's benefits outweigh the risk depends on where you live and your puppy's lifestyle. For example, Lyme disease is common in some areas of the United States and not in others, so your vet may not recommend this vaccine. Leptospirosis is a concern in some areas, but the disease hasn't been reported for decades in other parts of the United States. Bordetella (kennel cough) is a flu-like illness that your dog may be exposed to if you board him or take him to dog shows, but he may not be in danger if you don't go to places with large numbers of other dogs. If your veterinarian recommends these vaccines, be sure to discuss the reasons why your puppy should—or shouldn't—have them.

The Booster Dilemma

Most veterinary schools currently recommend that puppies receive their initial vaccines and then be given boosters a year later. After that, most recommend giving a booster every third year. To keep the level of vaccines as low as possible, many veterinarians set up a routine to give a rabies booster one year, a distemper booster the next, and a parvo booster the following year, and then back to rabies. Boosters of any kind are still controversial, and it is possible that in future years fewer or maybe even no boosters will be given.

The choices about which diseases to vaccinate against and how often to give boosters are important ones for the well-being of your puppy. A dedicated,

Some vaccines may be recommended based on where you live.

knowledgeable veterinarian who keeps up on the latest research about vaccine protocols is the very best defense for keeping your dog safe.

The Diseases
Bordetella (Kennel Cough)

The symptoms of bordetella are coughing, sneezing, hacking, and retching accompanied by nasal discharge usually lasting from a few days to several weeks. There are several disease-producing organisms responsible for this illness. The present vaccines are helpful but do not protect against all

Leptospirosis Vaccine

If your veterinarian recommends a vaccination against leptospirosis, be sure you have discussed this vaccine in-depth. This disease is a serious one, and animals who spend time in forested areas are mostly likely to be exposed to it. However, it is one of the vaccines that has had the most frequent reports of severe anaphylactic shock, which means your dog could stop breathing and could even die. The University of California at Davis School of Veterinary Medicine says that the incidence of severe reactions are most common in puppies and small-breed dogs. They conclude that "A careful risk-benefit analysis is recommended before considering vaccination of small-breed dogs at risk of exposure to leptospires."

strains. It usually is not life threatening, but in some instances can progress to bronchopneumonia. The disease is highly contagious, and the vaccination should be given routinely to dogs who come into contact with other dogs through boarding kennels, training classes, or visits to the groomer.

Coronavirus

Coronavirus is usually self-limiting and not life threatening. It was first noted in the late 1970s, about a year before parvovirus. The virus produces a yellow/brown stool and may be accompanied by depression, vomiting, and diarrhea.

Distemper

Distemper is often a fatal disease. If a puppy does recover, he is subject to severe nervous disorders. The virus attacks the entire body and resembles a bad cold with a fever. It can cause runny nose and eyes and gastrointestinal disorders, including a poor appetite, vomiting, and diarrhea. The virus is carried by raccoons, foxes, wolves, mink, and other dogs. Unvaccinated puppies are very susceptible.

Hepatitis

The hepatitis virus is most serious in very young dogs. It is spread by contact with an infected animal through feces or urine. The virus affects the liver and kidneys and is characterized by high fever, depression, and lack of appetite. Recovered animals may be afflicted with chronic illness.

Leptospirosis

Leptospirosis is a bacterial disease transmitted by contact with the urine of an infected dog, rat, or any other wildlife. It produces severe fever, depression, jaundice, and internal bleeding and was fatal before the vaccine was developed. Recovered dogs can be carriers, and the disease can be transmitted from dogs to humans. Unfortunately, there are several strains of leptospirosis, and vaccinations usually protect against only two.

Lyme Disease

Lyme disease was first diagnosed in the US in 1976 in Lyme, CT, in people who lived near areas that had deer ticks. Symptoms may include acute lameness, fever, swelling of joints, and loss of appetite. Your veterinarian can tell you if you live in a high-risk area.

Parvovirus

Parvovirus was first noted in the late 1970s and can still be a fatal disease. However, with proper vaccinations, early diagnosis, and prompt treatment, it is manageable. It attacks the bone marrow and intestinal tract. The symptoms include depression, loss of appetite, vomiting, diarrhea, and collapse. Immediate medical attention is essential.

Rabies

Rabies is shed in an animal's saliva and is carried by raccoons, skunks, foxes, other dogs, and cats. It attacks the nervous system, resulting in paralysis and death. Rabies can be transmitted to people and is always fatal. The only true test for rabies involves euthanizing the animal.

EXTERNAL PARASITES

There are many types of external parasites, and your puppy is susceptible, especially if he spends a lot of time outdoors or around other pets. The best way to deal with these buggy creatures is to keep one step ahead of them at all times.

The cheyletiella mite causes intense itching.

Be vigilant about checking your pup's coat, especially after he's been playing outside. There are also products on the market available through your veterinarian that will keep the creepy crawlers away. An ounce of prevention is worth a pound of cure—this is especially true when it comes to keeping your pup bug-free.

Cheyletiella

This mite causes intense itching and is diagnosed by skin scraping. It lives in the outer layers of the skin in dogs, cats, rabbits, and humans. Yellow-gray scales may be found on the back and the rump, top of the head, and the nose of dogs who are suffering from this particular type of mite.

Demodectic Mange

This mite is passed from the dam to her puppies. It often affects youngsters from three to ten months of age. Diagnosis is confirmed by skin scraping. Small areas of hair loss around the eyes, lips, and/or forelegs become visible. There is little itching unless there is a secondary bacterial infection.

Fleas

These pests are not only a dog's worst enemy but also an enemy to you, your house, your yard, and your pocketbook.

Check your puppy for fleas and ticks after he's been outside.

Once fleas infiltrate the area, they can be very difficult to get rid of. Many dogs are allergic to a fleabite, and in some cases, it only takes one fleabite to start an allergic reaction. This can result in open sores or fleabite dermatitis. A heavy infestation of these pests can cause blood loss and then anemia, which can be fatal to tiny pups. Preventing flea infestation is the key.

If you aren't sure if your dog has fleas, place the pup on a solid, light-colored sheet or blanket. Comb his coat thoroughly, especially around the stomach, the armpits, and around the tail. (These out-of-the-way places are where fleas like to hide.) Then let him up. If there is any residue on the sheet, the brush, or the comb that looks like salt (which are flea eggs) and pepper (which are flea dirt or fecal matter), your dog has fleas.

If there is a flea infestation, no one product is going to correct the problem. Not only will the dog require treatment, but so will the environment. However, some products are not usable on young puppies, and treating fleas should be done under your veterinarian's guidance. Treat all pets in your household at the same time because fleas are easily passed from one to the other.

Adult fleas live on the dog, but their eggs drop off of the dog into the environment. There they go through four larval stages before reaching adulthood, when they are then able to jump back on your unsuspecting puppy. The cycle resumes and takes between 21 to 28 days under ideal conditions. Several environmental products are available that will kill both the adult fleas and the larvae.

Heartworm

Incidents of heartworm have been found in all 50 states. According to the American Heartworm Society, the highest infection rate in dogs occurs within 150 miles (241 km) of the Atlantic and Gulf coasts and along the Mississippi River.

Use a spray designed for outside use in the yard and a spray designated for inside use in your home. Carefully follow the directions on any product that you use.

Getting Rid of Fleas
- Vacuum rugs and furniture to get rid of flea eggs. Change the vacuum bag often so that fleas are not deposited back into the area later.
- Treat the area with flea killer.
- Wash the dog's bedding and blankets in hot soapy water and wash out all crates, doghouses, toys, etc., with disinfectant.
- Sweep all uncarpeted areas, including porches, sidewalks, and patios.
- Treat your yard with flea killer.
- Give your puppy a bath and apply topical flea preventive.
- Remember to reapply flea preventive to your dog as recommended.

Ringworm
Ringworm isn't really a worm but rather several different kinds of fungi that can affect dogs and humans. These very contagious fungi infest the skin and cause round, scaly, "ring-like" areas that are

very itchy. Because this is so contagious, immediately take your puppy to the vet for treatment and follow directions exactly to prevent the fungus from spreading.

Sarcoptic Mange

The mite characterized by sarcoptic mange is difficult to find on skin scrapings. The female mite burrows under the skin and lays her eggs, which hatch within a few days. Sarcoptic mange causes intense itching in dogs and may even be characterized by hair loss in its early stages. Sarcoptes are highly contagious to other dogs and to humans, although they do not live long on humans.

Ticks

Ticks are known carriers of disease for both animals and humans. They carry Rocky Mountain spotted fever and Lyme disease and can cause tick paralysis. These eight-legged oval insects will bury their heads in your puppy's skin and live off his blood. You can remove them with tweezers, using a slow, twisting motion, and pulling out the head. Although using a flea preventive can help repel some ticks, it is not totally effective. Dogs should be checked for ticks regularly, especially if they have been in wooded areas or tall brush.

INTERNAL PARASITES

Worms—yuck! Yes, internal parasites are disgusting and can also be extremely dangerous for your puppy. They can be found in very young puppies because many are passed from mother to offspring, either in the womb or through

One of the best ways to prevent internal parasites in your puppy is to keep your yard free of feces.

nursing. They are also dangerous because you can't actually see all of them, and many times pups will not show any obvious symptoms until very ill.

Intestinal parasites are more prevalent in some areas than others. Climate, soil, and contamination are big factors that contribute to the incidence of intestinal parasites. How does your puppy get these things? A dog with worms may defecate in the local park. Eggs are passed in the stool. Dogs sniff or walk through the feces and may get some on their coat or feet and lick it off. The best chance of your puppy remaining worm-free is to regularly pooper-scooper your yard and watch out for your puppy in public places where other dogs may be. Other good ways to avoid worms are to keep your puppy free of fleas, ticks,

and other external parasites, to check for worms regularly, and to have your veterinarian perform a fecal examination on your dog twice a year or more. Different types of worms require different treatments, so don't waste your money buying over-the-counter medication without first consulting your veterinarian.

Coccidia and Giardia

Protozoan infections coccidia and giardia usually affect puppies, especially where large numbers of puppies are brought together. Symptoms include diarrhea, weight loss, and lack of appetite. These infections are not always apparent upon fecal examination.

Heartworms

Heartworms are worms residing in the heart and adjacent blood vessels of the lungs. The worm produces microfilariae, which circulate in the bloodstream. It is possible for a dog to be infected with any number of worms that can be 6 to 14 inches (15 to 35 cm) long. It is a life-threatening disease that is expensive to treat and easily prevented. Depending on where you live, your veterinarian may recommend preventive medication to be given year-round, as well as an annual or semiannual blood test. The most common preventive is given once a month.

Hookworms

Hookworms are almost microscopic intestinal worms that can cause anemia, which could lead to serious problems, including death, in young puppies. If their mother has them, the puppies may be born with them, or they can be transmitted to humans through penetration of the skin.

Roundworms

Roundworms are spaghetti-like worms that can cause a potbellied appearance and dull coat, along with more severe symptoms, such as vomiting, diarrhea, and coughing. Puppies can acquire these in utero and through nursing. Both hookworms and roundworms may also be acquired through ingestion.

Tapeworms

Seldom apparent on fecal floatation, tapeworms are seen frequently as rice-like segments around the dog's anus and the base of the tail. Tapeworms are long, flat, ribbon-like, and segmented. Dogs

Spaying or neutering curbs some unwanted behaviors and promotes good health.

can acquire tapeworms in two ways: by ingesting the flea through licking and chewing, or through rabbits, rodents, and certain large game animals that serve as intermediate hosts for other species of tapeworms. If your puppy eats one of these infected hosts, he can acquire tapeworms.

Whipworms

Whipworms have a three-month life cycle and are not acquired through the puppy's mother. They cause intermittent diarrhea, usually with mucus. Whipworms are possibly the most difficult worm to eradicate because their eggs can last for years until the proper conditions enable them to mature. Whipworms are seldom seen in the stool.

SPAYING AND NEUTERING

When you purchased a pet-quality puppy from a breeder or adopted a puppy from a shelter, it was probably requested that you have your pet neutered or spayed. This is based on what is healthiest for your dog and what is most beneficial for the breed.

For purebred dogs, experienced and conscientious breeders devote many years to developing a bloodline. They make every effort to plan each breeding with regard to conformation, temperament, and health. This type of breeder performs the necessary testing (i.e., OFA, PennHip, CERF, testing for inherited blood disorders, thyroid, etc.) for their breed. Reputable breeders do not want the dogs they produce to be bred indiscriminately—an important concept. More and more effort is being made to breed healthier, better dogs.

Shelters and humane societies require that you spay or neuter your puppy because they see firsthand how vast the problem of pet overpopulation is and wish to spare any resulting puppy of such litters the pain of being placed in a shelter.

When to Spay/Neuter

You should spay your female pup at around six months of age; there are numerous benefits to this. Unspayed females are subject to mammary and ovarian cancer. In order to prevent mammary cancer, a female should be spayed prior to her first heat cycle. Later in life, an unspayed female may develop pyometra, a life-threatening uterine infection. Spaying is performed under a general anesthetic and is easy on the young dog. As you might expect, it is a little harder on an older dog, but that is no reason to deny your older girl future good health. The surgery removes the ovaries and uterus. It is important to remove all the ovarian tissue. If some is left, your dog could remain attractive to males.

Neutering the male at a young age will inhibit some characteristic male behavior that owners frown upon. Some boys may not lift their legs and mark territory if they are neutered at six months of age. Also, neutering at a young age has other benefits, such as lessening the chance of hormonal aggressiveness. Surgery involves removing the testicles from the scrotum. If your male has a retained testicle either in the abdomen or inguinal

A Weighty Matter

Some people worry that their dog may gain weight after being neutered or spayed. This is usually not the case. Most dogs are just as fit and active as they were before surgery. However, if you notice a weight gain, you need to decrease the dog's food intake and provide a little more exercise.

canal, he needs to be neutered before the age of two or three years. Unneutered males are at risk for testicular cancer, perineal fistulas, perianal tumors, and prostatic disease.

Intact males and females are prone to housetraining accidents as well. Females urinate more frequently before, during, and after heat cycles, and males tend to mark territory if there is a female in heat. Males may show the same behavior to a visiting dog or guests. Spaying or neutering curbs these behaviors and promotes good health.

RECOGNIZING TROUBLE

Most puppy owners are lucky; their pups live healthy lives and never require more than an annual trip to the veterinarian for booster shots. But dogs, like all other animals, may contract problems and diseases that need professional treatment. It is a very bad idea to attempt to diagnose a problem without the advice of a veterinarian. A relatively common problem, such as diarrhea,

might be caused by nothing more than a puppy pigging out on leftovers or eating something unusual. Conversely, it could be the first indication of a potentially fatal disease. Your veterinarian is the only one qualified to make the correct diagnosis. Taking your puppy to the veterinarian is the most responsible and humane thing you can do for your dog. He will thank you for it.

The following symptoms, especially if they accompany each other or progressively add to earlier symptoms, indicate that you should visit the veterinarian right away.

Allergic Reactions
If your puppy swells up (especially in the face) or becomes ill after eating

Certain symptoms, like crying when being touched, require a trip to the vet.

something or receiving a bite or sting from another animal or insect, you are probably seeing an allergic reaction. Seek treatment as soon as possible.

Crying When Eliminating
This might be a minor problem caused by constipation, but it could be more serious and indicative of an internal infection or blockage, especially if the pup cries when urinating as well.

Crying When Touched
Obviously, a puppy might yelp if you do not handle him with care. However, if your

dog cries even when lifted gently, there may be an internal problem that becomes apparent when pressure is applied to a given area of the body. If there is also an extended abdomen, pain, or lameness in any of the joints, take your pet to the vet.

Cuts or Wounds

Most cuts or scrapes can be easily treated by washing the affected area and applying an antibiotic ointment. However, if your puppy has suffered a wound that will not stop bleeding with direct pressure, you need to go to the veterinarian for further treatment.

Diarrhea

Many factors, including change of environment, change of diet, or stress, can cause diarrhea. If it lasts more than 48 hours or if blood is seen in the feces, something is wrong and your puppy should be taken to the vet immediately.

Eye Injuries

If your puppy suffers from any sort of eye injury, your veterinarian should be contacted immediately.

Fainting or Seizures

Seizing or fainting can indicate a number of disorders, some very serious. If your puppy has a seizure or suddenly collapses, first prevent the pup from being injured as best you can; then contact your vet immediately.

General Listlessness

All puppies have days when they do not seem their usual energetic, mischievous

Your puppy's eyes should be clear and free of discharge.

selves. However, if your puppy seems overly tired, restless, or aggressive, or is displaying unusual behavior, like hiding from you, then there is a problem. This general malaise or change in personality may or may not accompany other symptoms. There are many diseases that can develop internally without displaying obvious clinical signs. Blood, fecal, and other tests are needed in order to identify the disorder before it reaches an advanced state.

Refusing Food

Generally, puppies are greedy creatures and will eat almost anything you offer. Some may be fussier than others, but no puppy will usually refuse more than one meal. If your pup goes for a number of hours without showing any interest in food, then something is decidedly behind this behavior and the dog should be taken for an examination.

Respiratory Problems

Prolonged coughing, wheezing, or any other indication that your puppy is having trouble breathing is a sign of a problem. Check for a blockage, then immediately call your veterinarian.

Runny Eyes and/or Nose

If your pup's eyes and nose are weepy, they should quickly clear up if the puppy is placed in a warm environment and away from any drafts. If they do not, and especially if a mucous discharge is seen,

these symptoms must be diagnosed by your veterinarian.

Vomiting

All puppies vomit from time to time, and it is not necessarily a sign of illness. However, continued vomiting is a clear sign of a problem. It may be a blockage in the pup's intestinal tract, it may be induced by worms, or it could indicate any number of diseases.

GIVING MEDICATION

It can be very frustrating to try to get your squirmy little pup to swallow a pill, but it is not impossible. Following are a few tips that can help make it easier for everyone.

When giving a pill, never underestimate the power of treats. Many dogs love cheese, so wrap the pill in cheese and your dog will probably wolf it down. If cheese isn't your dog's weakness, almost anything else will work. Peanut butter, bread, a bit of hot dog, or a soft dog biscuit are good hiding places for pills.

Liquid medicine can be a little harder. It is easiest to use a syringe into which the medication can be measured. Place the tip into the side of your puppy's mouth by the back teeth. Squirt the medication in, and then hold your puppy's muzzle shut so that he cannot spit it out; stroke your dog's throat so that he will swallow.

Eye medication should be given as quickly as possible. Give the puppy something to occupy him, hold his head, spread the eyelids, and apply the medication.

If your pup refuses more than one meal, take him to the vet.

TAKING YOUR PUPPY'S TEMPERATURE

The normal canine temperature is 99.5° to 102.5°F (37.5° to 39°C). Taking your dog's temperature is a good way to detect illness. To take your puppy's temperature accurately, use a rectal thermometer. Obviously, it is best to buy one for canine use only. Lubricate the tip of the thermometer using petroleum jelly. Kneel alongside your puppy or place him on your lap. Lift the tail gently and rotate the thermometer gently into the rectum, only going in about an inch or two (2 to 5 cm). It will take two minutes to get an accurate reading on a regular thermometer (less time with a digital), so praise and distract your puppy until time is up. If the temperature is too high or low, call your veterinarian and report your readings, along with any other symptoms.

CAPILLARY REFILL TIME

It is important to know how gums look when your puppy is healthy so that you can recognize potential problems. There are one or two breeds, like Chow Chows, that have black gums and a black tongue, which is normal for them. Generally, however, a healthy dog will have bright pink gums. Pale gums are an indication of shock or anemia and should be considered an emergency. Likewise, any yellowish tint is an indication of a sick dog. To check a dog's capillary refill time (CRT), press your thumb against the gums. The gum will turn white but should refill and turn to normal color within one

Check This

Health care does not end with vaccinations. It is very important to take your dog to the vet for an annual checkup, which includes booster vaccinations, a check for intestinal parasites, and a blood test for heartworm. The annual physical is good preventive medicine. Through early diagnosis and subsequent treatment of potential problems, your dog can maintain a longer and better life.

or two seconds. Your pup's CRT is very important—if the refill time is slow and the puppy is feeling poorly, you should call the veterinarian immediately.

HEART RATE, PULSE, AND RESPIRATION

You can take your dog's heart rate by pressing your fingertips on his chest. Count for ten seconds and then multiply by six to obtain the rate per minute. Normal heart rates range from about 50 beats per minute in the larger breeds to 130 beats per minute in the smaller ones. A normal pulse rate is the same as a heart rate and is taken at the femoral artery, which is located on the insides of both rear legs. Respiration should be observed, and depending on the size of the dog, should be about 10 to 30 breaths per minute.

8

PUPPY
FIRST AID

t is a good idea to always be prepared for an emergency. As you may well know, puppies are ingenious at getting into any and all sorts of trouble. Even if you have puppy-proofed your house as recommended, there is always the possibility that something may happen. Always keep a first-aid kit nearby, and have the numbers of your veterinarian, emergency clinic, and poison control center near the telephone.

PUPPY FIRST-AID KIT

Before you bring your puppy home, you should put together a first-aid kit, which should include:

- Adhesive bandaging tape
- Antibacterial soap
- Antibiotic ointment or powder
- Blanket or towels
- Cotton balls
- Eyewash
- Gauze rolls
- Hydrogen peroxide
- Milk of magnesia
- Muzzle—panty hose or stretchable gauze could make a muzzle
- Petroleum jelly
- Rubbing alcohol
- Scissors
- Thermometer
- Tweezers
- Vital information card: phone numbers for vet, clinic, etc.

EMERGENCY SITUATIONS

There are things that you can do to help your dog if he ever suffers from any of the following problems.

Accidents

Many traffic accidents can be easily prevented by making sure that your puppy is always in a fenced area or on leash. If an accident does occur, remember not to panic. First, get your dog to a safe area. He may be in pain or in shock, so make an emergency muzzle so that you don't get bitten while you are trying to help. Is the dog conscious or unconscious? Are there any obvious injuries, like bleeding or broken limbs? Even if there are no obvious injuries, your dog may still be injured internally.

Try to get another person to help you lift the dog onto a blanket, but with no more movement than absolutely necessary. Use the blanket as a stretcher, and

Keep a first-aid kit handy in case of accidents.

How to Make an Emergency Muzzle

An injured dog may be frightened or in pain and may not even recognize his owner. Use an emergency muzzle to protect yourself from being bitten when you try to help.

- Use a strip of cloth, bandage, nylon stocking, or leash to make a muzzle quickly.
- Make a large loop by tying a loose knot in the middle of the strip of cloth.
- Hold the ends up, one in each hand.
- Slip the loop over the dog's muzzle and lower jaw, just behind the nose.
- Quickly tighten the loop so that the dog's mouth cannot open.
- Tie the ends under the lower jaw.
- Make a knot and pull the ends back on each side of the face and under the ears to the back of the head.

Try practicing this when your dog is calm and not injured so that you are ready for any emergency.

carry the dog to your car for immediate transport to your veterinarian or emergency clinic. Even without external injuries, the dog should still be x-rayed for broken bones or internal damage.

Bites

If your dog gets bitten, try to stop any bleeding, wash the area, and determine the severity of the situation. Some bites may be superficial and easily treated, while others may need immediate attention. However, most should be seen by a veterinarian, and some may require antibiotics or stitches.

Bleeding

Bleeding can result from any accident, such as a ripped dewclaw, a toenail cut too short, a puncture wound, or a laceration. If your puppy is bleeding, apply a clean pressure bandage and check every 15 to 20 minutes to ensure

that it is not too tight. Styptic powder can stop the flow of blood from a small cut on the dewclaw or toenail. Clean the wound with antiseptic. If the wound is deep or does not stop bleeding, take your pup to the veterinarian immediately.

Bloat

Bloat (gastric dilatation volvulus) is a life-threatening veterinary emergency. No one knows for certain what causes this painful and fast-acting condition, but when it happens, the dog's stomach twists, trapping fluids and gas within it. This causes the dog severe pain and unless treated immediately with emergency surgery, can result in death. Deep-chested breeds and large- or giant-sized dogs are most susceptible, such as the Great Dane, German Shepherd Dog, and Saint Bernard.

Signs that your dog may be bloated include retching without vomiting, excessive salivation, weakness, swelling of the abdomen, abnormal rapid breathing, and increased heart rate. Because death can occur within hours, rush your puppy to the vet immediately if you see these symptoms.

Although the exact cause of bloat is not known, controlling your dog's food intake may help prevent the condition. Feed several small meals throughout the day instead of one large meal, and don't let your dog exercise one hour before or after eating.

Cardiac Arrest

If you realize that your dog is not breathing, you should have someone call the veterinarian and plan for transportation to an emergency facility immediately. If your dog does not have a heartbeat or spontaneous respiration, you can perform CPR.

CPR may help save your puppy's life. This will require two people—one person to breathe for the dog and the other to try to establish a heart rhythm. Mouth-to-mouth resuscitation requires two initial breaths, one to one-and-a-half seconds in duration. After the initial breaths, breathe for the dog once after every five chest compressions. To do this, inhale, cover the dog's nose with your mouth, and exhale gently into the dog's mouth. You should see his chest expand. Sometimes, pulling the puppy's tongue forward stimulates respiration. You should ventilate the dog 12 to 20 times per minute.

The person who is managing the chest compressions should make sure that the dog is lying on his right side and should

Deep-chested breeds like the Great Dane are at risk for bloat.

place one hand on either side of the dog's chest directly over the heart (between the fourth and fifth ribs, usually at the point of the flexed elbow). The number of chest compressions administered depends on the size of the patient—about 80 compressions per minute for a puppy. Check for spontaneous heartbeat and/or respiration while you are performing CPR, and if they are present, discontinue resuscitation and monitor the patient.

Choking

If your dog is choking, see if any foreign object is visible. If so, remove it. If no object is visible, you can perform the

Heimlich maneuver on your dog. Wrap your arms tightly around your dog's belly just under the rib cage. Give one quick forceful squeeze, and the object causing the obstruction should be expelled.

You can also try holding the puppy upside down to see if the object will become dislodged. Meanwhile, have someone call the veterinarian.

Drowning

Remove any debris from the puppy's mouth and swing the dog, holding him upside down. Try to stimulate respiration by pulling the tongue forward. Administer CPR if necessary and call your veterinarian. Do not give up working on your dog, and go to the vet as soon as possible. Be sure to wrap the dog in blankets or towels to prevent shock.

Electrocution

Unfortunately, puppies have been known to chew on electrical wires and get a shock. If this happens, turn off the current before touching the dog. Check for a normal heart rate and that the dog is breathing. Administer mouth-to-mouth resuscitation or CPR if necessary. Go to the veterinarian as soon as possible because electrocution can cause internal damage that will need medical treatment.

Heatstroke

Heatstroke is a serious emergency—and can usually be prevented. Dogs are not able to cool off by sweating as humans can. Their only way to cool off is by panting and radiation of heat from the skin's surface. When exposed

Heat Problems

Although it's been said many times before, many people don't realize how quickly a car can overheat, even with the windows cracked open. Never leave a dog unattended in a car. Also, short-nosed breeds, like Bulldogs and Pugs, and obese or infirm dogs should not be left outside for long periods in hot weather and should only exercise in the early morning or evening when the temperature is cooler.

to high temperatures, high humidity, or poor ventilation, dogs can suffer from heatstroke very quickly, especially brachycephalic (short-nosed) breeds, like Bulldogs or Pugs.

The signs of heatstroke are rapid, shallow breathing, rapid heartbeat, a temperature above 104°F (40°C), and collapse. The dog needs to be cooled down as quickly as possible and treated by a veterinarian. If possible, spray your pup with cool water or cover him with cool, wet towels. Pack ice around the head, neck, and groin, and let the dog slowly drink cool, not cold, water. Monitor his temperature and stop the aforementioned procedure as soon as the temperature reaches 103°F (39°C). However, continue monitoring because you do not want it to elevate again or drop below 100°F (37°C). The best thing to do for your puppy is to get professional help as soon as possible.

Poisoning

Hopefully, you have followed this book's advice and have sufficiently puppy-proofed your home. However, puppies do have a way of getting into things that they shouldn't.

If your puppy eats or drinks something poisonous, call your vet immediately. Be prepared to give the weight and age of your puppy and the quantity of toxin consumed, and have the bottle handy to read off the ingredients. If you can't reach the vet, you can call the National Animal Poison Control Center (1-800-222-1222).

Symptoms of poisoning include muscle trembling and weakness, increased salivation, vomiting, and loss of bowel control. There are numerous household toxins, plants, and pesticides that can be harmful to your puppy, so be sure to keep a careful eye and act immediately if you suspect he has eaten something poisonous.

Seizure

Some dogs are prone to seizures, which may also be a secondary symptom of an underlying medical condition. Make sure

Make sure all of the plants in your house are not toxic to dogs.

the dog is in a safe place and cannot hurt himself. Do not try to handle the dog's mouth or you may get bitten. Notify your veterinarian if your puppy has a seizure, fit, or convulsion of any kind so that he can be checked for further problems.

Shock

Shock is a life-threatening condition that requires immediate veterinary care. It can occur after an injury or a severe scare. Other causes of shock are hemorrhage, fluid loss, infection, poison, adrenal insufficiency, cardiac failure, and anaphylaxis. The symptoms are a weak, rapid pulse, shallow breathing, dilated pupils, low temperature, and muscle weakness. The puppy's capillary refill time (CRT) will also be slow. Keep the dog warm and go to the veterinary clinic immediately. Timing is critical to survival.

Swallowing Foreign Objects

There is one thing that puppy owners will learn very quickly—it doesn't have to be food for your puppy to swallow it. Dogs have been known to swallow anything, including socks, clothing, panty hose, toys, and plastic. Sometimes these items may pass through the puppy's body without incident, but other times he may not be so lucky. The object may get stuck in the intestinal tract or stomach and sometimes needs to be removed surgically. If you suspect that your puppy has swallowed a foreign object, contact your veterinarian. Depending on what it is, the vet may either tell you to induce vomiting or to come to the clinic for

further treatment. Don't induce vomiting until you talk to your vet—some objects may do more damage coming back up.

Walks on the Wild Side

Every now and then, your puppy could have a run-in with another animal—and the outcome may not be pleasant. The following information will help if your puppy has a problem with a member of another species.

Bee Stings

Bees and wasps will leave an embedded stinger in your puppy's skin. Remove the stinger with tweezers and apply ice if the area swells. Some people swear that a paste of baking soda and water will help to ease discomfort; others use milk of magnesia or ammonia to soothe the area. Some dogs will have an allergic reaction to bee stings and will experience severe swelling in the face or throat. If this happens, urgent medical care is necessary.

Porcupine Quills

Having a run-in with a porcupine can be one of the biggest mistakes your puppy may make. Porcupine quills have backward-pointing scale-like hooks that hold them firmly in the flesh, making them painful and difficult to remove. If your puppy has been really pricked, it is best to go to the vet to get them removed. A vet may administer anesthetic, so the dog may escape some of the pain. You can try to get the quills out yourself if there are only a few. Wear rubber gloves to protect your hands and try to soothe your puppy—these things really hurt! With a pair of needle-nose or blunt-nose pliers, grab a quill as close to the dog's coat as possible. Pull steadily until it comes out. Once you get the quills out, apply a topical antiseptic to prevent infection.

Skunks

Most puppies will investigate anything. Your puppy's curiosity will be peaked by that black-and-white animal over there, and next thing you know—skunked! First,

don't let your dog inside the house—that smell can be almost impossible to get rid of. Check the pup's eyes for any redness or irritation, and if there is any, wash the eyes with cool water. Then it's bath time, preferably outside under the garden hose. Shampoo and rinse him thoroughly. Unfortunately, this is sometimes just not enough to get rid of the odor. Pet owners recommend rinsing your dog with tomato juice; an over-the-counter skunk odor remover; or a solution of baking soda, liquid soap, and hydrogen peroxide.

Snake Bites

It is good to know if any poisonous snakes are in your area so that you can be extra careful when walking with your dog. If your puppy is bitten and exhibits any swelling, trembling, drooling, vomiting, excitability, dilated pupils, or collapses, apply an ice pack to the wound and do your best to stem the flow of blood if there is any. If the bite is on the leg, apply ice and wrap a bandage tightly around the wound. Contact your veterinarian at once.

Toads

Toads are poisonous if ingested and quite deadly to dogs. You should find out if these critters live in your area and what they look like.

9

FEEDING AND NUTRITION

As a puppy owner, you'll discover that the one thing your puppy loves the most (besides you, of course) is food. Good nutrition is a necessary requirement in a puppy's life. Providing your puppy with the proper diet is one of the most important aspects of dog care. By carefully researching which diet is best for your puppy, you can ensure his good health.

A PUPPY'S NUTRITIONAL NEEDS

Puppies may have individual nutritional needs depending on the breed group to which they belong. Each breed has different activity levels, hereditary conditions, genetic makeups, and original functions, so each will require a specialized diet to fit these needs.

The Herding Group

This group needs an abundance of protein because it uses up a lot of energy in its everyday work. Hip dysplasia is prevalent in several breeds, such as the Collie and the Shetland Sheepdog, and slowing down the puppy's growth rate can help reduce the symptoms. Also, German Shepherd Dogs tend to suffer from chronic intermittent diarrhea resulting from an intestinal immune deficiency, so fat calories should be monitored carefully.

The Hound Group

This group is prone to intestinal problems and requires a highly digestible diet. A diet high in ground rice, oats, and barley can help provide a balance of fiber and carbohydrates to improve gastrointestinal

health. Also, small hounds, like Beagles and Dachshunds, can suffer from bone and joint problems as well as obesity.

When you purchase your puppy, make sure the breeder discusses all the health problems that exist in the breed along with what you can do to nutritionally manage potential health problems.

The Non-Sporting Group

A generous supply of vitamins A and B and minerals such as copper and zinc can help this group of dogs that often suffers from skin and hair coat conditions. Dalmatians tend to have uric acid calculi problems, so puppies should be given a low-purine diet. (Purines are a type of protein known to promote urinary stones in Dalmatians.) Breeds like Poodles and Bichons Frises tend to have problems with periodontal disease, so special care should be taken to feed them kibble to help reduce tartar buildup.

The Sporting Group

As a whole, this group needs extra calories for energy and performance. You should look for a dog food with higher amounts of vitamin and mineral fortification, as well as choline to help process nutrients into energy. Some Irish Setters are gluten intolerant, which can cause weight loss and diarrhea. Grains containing gluten—like wheat, barley, and oats—should be eliminated, and rice should be used as a substitute.

Also, Cocker Spaniels and some Golden Retrievers suffer from a low taurine level that can be responsive to supplementation. Several sporting breeds

Ask your breeder about any specific nutritional needs for your breed.

suffer from hip dysplasia. Slowing down the dog's growth rate as a puppy has a positive impact in reducing this hereditary disease.

The Terrier Group

Terriers are basically healthy dogs, but they require a lot of protein if they live a high-performance lifestyle. In this group, 75 percent of all Bedlington Terriers suffer from copper toxicosis or are genetic carriers of it. If your Bedlington puppy carries this disease, you must discuss with your breeder or veterinarian the best way to manage the copper levels in his diet.

The Toy Group

Due to their small size, the breeds in the Toy Group have their own set of problems that can be managed nutritionally. In general, small dogs put out more body heat per unit of body weight than larger breeds. By managing the levels of protein, you can make the most of your toy dog's food intake for energy. Toy dogs, especially Yorkshire Terriers, often suffer from hypoglycemia, or low blood sugar. Maintaining blood sugar levels can reduce the incidence of this problem.

The Working Group

This group commonly encounters heart and gastrointestinal problems, as well as bone and joint difficulties. Choose a dog food that is restricted in salt for heart health and that is high in fiber for digestibility. These breeds can also suffer from hereditary bone diseases like hip dysplasia. Again, slowing down the dog's growth as a puppy can help reduce the symptoms of these conditions.

WHAT TO FEED YOUR PUPPY

If you take a trip to your local pet emporium or supermarket, you cannot help but notice that there is an overwhelming selection of dog foods available. It can be confusing, to say the least, and makes it hard to choose which brand is best for your puppy. There are certain things you should know about commercial dog foods that will help you make the right decision. The more you educate yourself about what your puppy's nutritional needs are and how dog food is manufactured, the easier the decision will be.

Essential Nutrients

In order to stay healthy, there are six essential nutrients that all dogs in every stage of life need in varied amounts: carbohydrates, fat, minerals, protein, vitamins, and water.

Carbohydrates

- Carbohydrates provide energy and keep intestines functioning smoothly. Complex carbohydrates are fiber and sugar.
- Sources include corn, oats, wheat, rice, and barley.
- Possible fertility and whelping problems may result if the diet is lacking in carbohydrates.

Fat

- Fat supplies energy needed for the absorption of certain vitamins, provides insulation from the cold, and makes food tastier.

- Sources include meat, meat by-products, and vegetable oils such as safflower, olive, corn, or soybean.
- Dull coat and delayed healing of wounds result if the diet is lacking in fat.

Minerals

- Minerals provide strength to bone, ensure proper bone formation, maintain fluid balance as well as normal muscle and nerve function, transport oxygen in the blood, and produce hormones.
- Calcium, phosphorus, copper, iron, magnesium, selenium, potassium, zinc, and sodium are essential minerals.
- Poor growth, rickets, convulsions, anemia, hair loss, lethargy, kidney

Some toy dogs, like Yorkies, suffer from hypoglycemia.

problems, or muscle weakness result from mineral deficiency.

Protein

- Proteins can be burned as calories and stored as fat. They help with muscle growth, tissue repair, blood clotting, and the immune system.
- Sources include meat, fish, poultry, milk, cheese, yogurt, fish meal, and eggs.
- Weight loss, dull coat, a depressed immune system, and poor growth result if the diet is lacking in protein.

Vitamins

- Vitamins are divided into two groups: water soluble and fat soluble. Water-soluble vitamins pass through the body

in urine. Fat-soluble vitamins are stored in body tissue and can become toxic in excessive amounts. Vitamin A protects skin and promotes bone growth; vitamin B aids in metabolism; vitamin D aids in bone growth and increases calcium absorption; and vitamin K helps with blood clotting.
- Sources include fruits, vegetables, cereals, and the livers of most animals.
- Skin thickening, nerve decay, heart failure, weight loss, anorexia, anemia, scaly skin, fatty liver, rickets, muscle weakness, infertility, or hemorrhage may result if the diet is lacking in vitamins.

Water

- Water is the most important nutrient and makes up over 60 percent of a puppy's body.
- Water intake can come directly through drinking or can be released in the body when food is oxidized.
- Dehydration, which can lead to serious deterioration of organs and even death, results from insufficient amounts of water.

Got Beef?

Unlike cats, dogs are not true carnivores and can exist on a vegetarian diet. They can convert vegetable fat and protein into the ingredients that they need to perform bodily functions. However, you should consult a veterinarian before switching your dog to a vegetarian diet, because it is a lot of work to maintain balanced nutrition.

TYPES OF COMMERCIAL DOG FOOD

Pick a dog food specially formulated for puppies that will ensure the proper nutrition for the pup's developing organ systems. There are three types of dog food available—dry, canned, and semi-moist—and all of them have good and bad points. You must choose the type that best fits your puppy's needs.

Dry Food

- **Pros:** Least expensive; can be left in bowl for longer periods of time; helps control tartar.
- **Cons:** Least appealing to dogs.

Canned Food

- **Pros:** Most appealing to dogs; high water content helps hydrate dogs; can be used in combination with dry foods to make diet more palatable.
- **Cons:** Spoils quickly; expensive; requires more to be fed because energy content is relatively low, especially for large breeds.

Semi-Moist Food

- **Pros:** Will not spoil at room temperature and comes in prepackaged servings.
- **Cons:** Contains large amounts of sugar and preservatives in order to maintain freshness without refrigeration.

READING LABELS

There are two agencies that work together in regulating pet food labels. The first agency, the Association of American Feed Control Officials (AAFCO), is a non-governmental agency made up of state and federal officials from all over

Water, Water, Everywhere

Water is the most important of all nutrients, and all dogs must retain a water balance. This means that their total intake of water should be in balance with the total output. Make sure that your puppy has access to cool, clean water at all times.

the United States. It establishes pet food regulations that cover areas like guaranteed analysis, nutritional adequacy statements, and feeding directions. Each state decides whether or not to enforce AAFCO's regulations. Most do; however, some do not.

The second agency, the Food and Drug Administration Center for Veterinary Medicine, establishes and enforces standards for all animal feed. This federal agency oversees aspects of labeling that cover proper identification of product, net quantity statements, and the list of ingredients.

Learn how to read dog food labels. Slight changes in wording can make the difference between a quality dog food and one that may not be what it seems.

Product Name

Specific words used in the name can indicate what is in the food and what is not. For example, a name like "Beef Dog Food" must contain at least 95-percent beef, but if it is called "Beef Formula for Dogs," it is required to contain a minimum of only 25-percent beef. Other words like "dinner," "platter," "nuggets," or "entrée" fall under this 25 percent minimum requirement.

Another word to watch for is "with." A dog food called "Dog Food With Beef" must contain only a minimum of 3-percent beef. The word "with" was originally supposed to highlight extra ingredients, but recent amendments to AAFCO regulations now allow the word to be used in the product name. The word "flavored" can be deceiving because it means that only a sufficient amount of flavoring needs to be added for it to be detectable. "Beef-Flavored Dog Food" may not include any beef at all and may only be flavored with very small amounts of beef by-products.

Truth in Advertising

Although dog food labels tell you a lot about a product, there is a lot they don't tell you. For example, some wording used on labels can be misleading. Foods that use the words "gourmet" or "premium" are not required to contain any higher-quality ingredients than any other product. Products that claim to be "all-natural" are not required to be. Some might think that this means the food is minimally processed or contains no artificial ingredients, but this is not necessarily true. In fact, all dog foods must

Make sure that your puppy has access to cool, clean water at all times.

contain some chemically synthesized ingredients in order to be deemed complete and balanced.

Ingredient List

Each ingredient contained in the food will be listed in descending order according to weight, but the quality of the ingredient is not required to be listed. For the best results, look for animal-based proteins to be high on the list, such as beef, beef by-products, chicken, chicken by-products, lamb, lamb meal, fish meal, and egg. However, read carefully because some manufacturers will manipulate the weight of products in order to place them higher or lower on the list. For example, they may divide the grains into different categories, like wheat flour and whole ground wheat, in order to lower the weight and make it seem less prominent on the ingredient list.

What Are By-Products?

What exactly are meat by-products and meal? Actual meat is considered to be the clean flesh of a slaughtered mammal and is limited to the part of the striated muscle that is skeletal or found in the tongue, diaphragm, heart, or esophagus. Meat by-products are the non-rendered lean parts other than the meat, which includes, but is not limited to, the lungs, spleen, kidney, bone, blood, stomach, intestines, necks, feet, and undeveloped eggs. Meat and bonemeal is the rendered product or mammal tissue, which includes bone, hair hood, horn, hide trimming, manure, and stomach. The ingredients in dog food can vary widely, so be informed about what your puppy is actually eating.

Guaranteed Analysis

The guaranteed analysis states the minimum amount of crude protein and crude fat, as well as the maximum amount percentage of moisture (water) and crude fiber. The word "crude" refers to the method of testing the product, not the quality of the nutrient. Sometimes, manufacturers will list other nutrients

Learning to read the food label can help ensure you are giving your puppy a quality commerical food.

Net Quantity Statement

The net quantity statement shows the weight of the food in the bag or can in pounds and ounces as well as metric weight. Be careful because some companies use 30-pound (14-kg) bags and then only put 25 pounds (11 kg) of food inside.

Feeding Instructions

The feeding instructions on the dog food label are only suggestions; some dogs will eat more, some will eat less. Also, they are the amounts needed for the entire day, so you can divide it up the best way for your puppy. If you are not sure how much to feed, start off with the suggested amount and increase or decrease as necessary.

HOMEMADE DIETS

There seems to be a debate about whether a homemade diet is better for your dog than manufactured dog food. The downside to a homemade diet is that you need to be very careful to ensure that you are providing your puppy with all the required nutrients. It also takes a lot of time, effort, and energy to cook a proper diet for your dog on a daily basis.

Those who are in favor of a homemade diet believe that commercial dog foods contain contaminated and unhealthy ingredients and feel that it is worth the effort to give their puppy a home-cooked meal. If you have the time and the money and believe that it is important to feed your dog a homemade diet, consult your veterinarian, who can give you a reputable and nutritionally balanced

like ash or calcium, although they are not required to do so.

The feeding instructions on the dog food label are only suggestions; some dogs will eat more, some will eat less.

Nutritional Adequacy Statement

This statement is important because it states what life stage the product is formulated for, such as growth, reproduction, maintenance, senior, or all life stages. For developing puppies, look for the product that is especially formulated for growth. It should also tell you whether the product is "complete and balanced" or "complementary." Complete and balanced means that it contains all the ingredients that your dog will need on a daily basis and it can be a meal by itself. Complementary means that it is not intended to be used alone and must be added to another product to create a complete meal.

recipe. Although millions of dogs exist and stay healthy on commercially prepared dog food, the ultimate decision is yours.

FEEDING YOUR PUPPY

If you are lucky, the breeder from whom you obtained your puppy will have given you a diet sheet, which will help you immensely with your feeding chores. A diet sheet will typically tell you the type of food your puppy has been eating, when he eats, and how to increase food intake as he ages. Some breeders will even include enough food to get you through a day or two. If possible, you should follow this original feeding schedule closely and use the same brand of puppy food for the first few months. This will help avoid any stomach upsets or diarrhea. If you would like to change the brand of food that your puppy is eating, do so gradually, slowly mixing the old food with the new food over a period of time until the old food is totally replaced.

If no diet sheet was provided for you, you will have to use the information available about dog food and choose one that is specially formulated for puppies. It should indicate that it is a growth formula. If you are undecided about which brand to choose, your veterinarian can make a recommendation.

How will you know if you have made the right choice? First, look at your puppy's stool. It should be small and firm, not too loose or too dry. A large amount of stool means that the food is not being digested. Although it may take a few months, a puppy eating a nutritious diet

If you have the time and do your research, a homemade diet could be an option for your puppy.

will have all the signs of good health, including a glossy coat, high energy, and bright eyes.

When to Feed

Start off with light, frequent meals because your puppy's stomach is so small. If the breeder has included a feeding schedule with your diet sheet, you should follow that as closely as possible and make increases or decreases as recommended. If no feeding schedule accompanied your puppy, set one up right away.

At four months of age or younger, a puppy should be fed four times a day. From four to six months of age, you can reduce the feedings to three, and after six months, you can start feeding once or twice a day, depending on your schedule. You should always feed at the same time of day, starting out with breakfast, lunch, mid-afternoon snack, and dinner, which should be served an hour before bedtime. Take your pup outside to "go potty" as soon as the meal is finished.

Some people recommend "free feeding," which means leaving food out for the puppy to nibble on all day. This makes it harder to judge exactly how much the dog has eaten and to predict when the dog needs to go outside to eliminate. It also could lead to overeating because many puppies will eat out of boredom. It is best to put the food down for your puppy for a limited time, then take the food away when the time is up. Your puppy will adjust quickly to the schedule, and you'll have more control over the amount consumed.

Will Work for Food

For puppies, food can be an important and effective training tool. A treat can be just the right motivation to encourage your pup to sit, come to you, follow you on leash—almost any behavior is more fun with a treat for a reward.

How Much to Feed

If you don't know the puppy's prior feeding schedule, you will have to figure out how much to feed him. Start by following the directions on the dog food label and increasing or decreasing the amount as needed. Put down the recommended amount for your puppy's age and take it away after a period of time. If your puppy eats the food quickly and leaves nothing, you need to increase the amount. If there is leftover food, you may have to decrease the amount or feed smaller meals more frequently.

Giving your puppy the proper amount of food is very important, especially for large- or giant-breed puppies. These dogs, who are usually over 65 pounds (29 kg) when mature, can suffer from skeletal abnormalities, such as hip dysplasia, hypertropic osteodystrophy, and osteochondritis dissecans if they grow too fast. These problems are characterized by improper development of joints or bones and can cause lameness. Some researchers also say that too much calcium in a puppy's diet can interfere with normal bone and cartilage development.

Although these problems have a lot to do with heredity, they can be nutritionally

Free feeding could lead to overeating.

They're Sweet Enough!

It may seem harmless to feed your puppy sweets, but chocolate can cause your dog to become seriously ill or even die. The two chemicals in chocolate, caffeine and theobromine, overstimulate the puppy's nervous system, especially in small dogs—10 ounces (283 g) of chocolate can kill a 12-pound (5-kg) dog! Symptoms of chocolate poisoning include restlessness, vomiting, increased heart rate, seizure, and coma. If your dog has ingested chocolate, call the ASPCA Poison Control Center (888-426-4435), and get your puppy to the veterinarian immediately.

managed. Be sure to talk with your breeder and your veterinarian about how to handle these problems if you have any questions.

Although they are not as susceptible to orthopedic problems, medium-sized to small-sized breeds also need to have their weight monitored. All puppies can become obese if they eat too much, which can lead to health problems. Small breeds can also suffer from low blood sugar levels. All dogs need to have a nutritionally balanced diet in order to stay their healthiest.

Supplements

Healthy puppies who are fed a balanced diet will not need supplements. In fact, some veterinarians believe that supplementing your puppy's diet with extra vitamins and minerals can aggravate conditions like hip dysplasia and hereditary skin problems. The only time you should give your puppy any kind of supplements is under the direction of your veterinarian, and even then you should never exceed the prescribed amount.

Treats and Bones

Treats are a great way to encourage and reward your puppy for doing something well. There are plenty of treats available today that are not only tasty but also nutritious. Hard biscuits can help keep puppy teeth clean. Remember to consider treats as part of the dog's total food intake. Limit the amount of treats and be sure to feed only healthy snacks. Avoid giving table scraps because they usually just add to caloric intake. Obesity is a very serious health problem in dogs, so be sure to start your puppy off eating right.

Bones can help your puppy with the overwhelming need to chew. They will also keep his teeth clean and prevent him from becoming bored. Make sure you give your dog safe bones and toys that are made specially for dogs and that will not splinter or break into tiny pieces, which can be swallowed and become stuck in the intestinal tract or choke the pup. There are plenty of manufacturers that make safe, chewable, edible dog bones, so give your puppy something fun and safe as a special treat.

Fussy Eaters

Although it is rare in puppies, you will occasionally run into a fussy eater. Here are a few tips to get your puppy to chow down at mealtime. (Remember, however, that if your puppy refuses meals for more than a day, consult your veterinarian.)

- Don't beg your puppy to eat. This only reinforces getting attention for this behavior. Just put down the food at the regular mealtime and walk away. Take it away again in 30 minutes, whether or not the pup has eaten.
- Don't feed table scraps. Your puppy may be eating plenty, just eating the wrong kind of food.
- Make the meal more appetizing by adding warm water or gravy mix to dry kibble. This should also stimulate his sense of smell, which will make him more hungry.

FEEDING DO'S AND DON'TS

To sum up, here's some do's and don'ts when it comes to feeding your puppy:

- Do provide puppy food made from a reputable manufacturer.
- Do have fresh water available for your puppy at all times.
- Do serve your puppy's food at room temperature.
- Do watch your puppy's weight.
- Do call your veterinarian if your puppy refuses to eat in a 24-hour period.
- Do feed your puppy nutritious snacks.
- Don't allow children to interfere while the puppy is eating.
- Don't offer spoiled or stale food to your puppy.
- Don't change your puppy's diet suddenly.
- Don't leave any uneaten canned or moist food out after your puppy is finished eating. Discard dry food at the end of each day.
- Don't allow your puppy to have brittle bones or unhealthy snacks.

Puppies aren't usually fussy eaters, so if he refuses meals for more than a day, consult your veterinarian.

10

GROOMING
YOUR PUPPY

Puppies rely on their owners to keep them clean and brushed, which can be done easily with regular grooming. Grooming is also important because it gives you a chance to inspect your dog and catch any skin or health problems before they start. Every dog, no matter what breed, will require grooming, and some breeds require more attention than others. Hopefully, you put some thought into the amount of time that you want to spend grooming your dog before you chose him and have taken home a breed that has the best coat type for you.

COAT TYPES

Each breed has a different coat that gives it a certain "look" and sets it

Bichons Frises have curly coats.

apart. There are lots of different looks from which to choose.

Of course, different coat types require different levels of care. The short coats will require little more than a daily brushing and an occasional bath; the longer coats or wiry coats may require special grooming procedures. Each dog needs a different amount of time and energy spent on grooming. But remember, every coat sheds to some degree.

Short

- **Short, Smooth Coat**—lies close to the body; Doberman Pinschers, Pugs, and Basenjis have this coat type.
- **Short, Wiry Coat**—thick, hard, and bristly; Wirehaired Dachshunds, all Schnauzers, and most terriers have this type of coat.
- **Short, Double Coat**—flat, straight, coarse hair on the outside and a soft, thin undercoat beneath it; Labrador Retrievers, smooth Chow Chows, and Rottweilers have this type of coat.

Long

- **Long, Double Coat**—long, straight, coarse outercoat and a very thick undercoat; Samoyeds, coated Chow Chows, and Collies have long, double coats.
- **Long, Coarse Coat**—softer undercoat mixed into the long, coarse coat; Shih Tzu, Lhasa Apsos, and Tibetan Terriers have this type of coat.
- **Curly Coat**—thick, dense curls; Bichons Frises and Poodles have this type of coat.
- **Long, Silky Coat**—very fine and has

little or no undercoat; Yorkshire Terriers, Maltese, and Silky Terriers have this coat type.

Other
- **Hairless**—some dogs, including the Chinese Crested and Xoloitzcuintli, are largely or completely hairless. Despite the lack of coat, they have very sensitive skin and need special attention.

GROOMING TOOLS
To keep your dog looking good, you need the right tools. There is a large selection of grooming equipment available for every coat type, but there are some universal tools that every owner should have for general grooming.
- **Bristle brush:** a medium-soft bristle brush will make a shorthaired coat gleam.
- **Doggy toothbrush and toothpaste:** Be sure to use toothpaste and toothbrushes that are made specifically for dogs.
- **Electric clippers:** Some breeds, like Poodles, have coats that need to be clipped every six to eight weeks.
- **Flea comb:** This is helpful in getting hard-to-reach spots and removing fleas or flea dirt.
- **Grooming glove:** This is great for dogs with short coats to loosen any dead hair and get rid of surface dirt.
- **Nail clippers:** Two types of clippers are available, guillotine and scissor.
- **Pin brush:** This has long, straight metal pins attached to a rubber backing and is used mostly on longer-haired breeds.
- **Rubber curry brush:** useful for times

Some people prefer the scissor-style nail clipper.

when your puppy has frolicked in something especially messy.
- **Scissors:** Blunt-nosed scissors are handy for trimming excess hair on feet, legs, tail, or anal region, as well as for trimming his whiskers.
- **Shampoo and conditioner made for dogs:** If you are unsure about what brand to buy, ask your breeder or veterinarian for a recommendation.
- **Slicker brush:** The wire bristles grasp and remove a dog's undercoat, helping to reduce shedding; it keeps the coat from becoming matted.

THE ROAD TO BEAUTY
Puppyhood is the best time to start grooming procedures because your dog will become used to the grooming routine and soon come to expect it as part of everyday life. This is especially true if you have a dog who requires extensive grooming or if you plan to show him. It is best to start out slowly so that the

dog doesn't become overwhelmed or frightened, and then build on grooming time until you have the whole routine down pat.

Grooming Table

If your puppy requires lots of grooming time, it is best to invest in a good grooming table. Your dog's leash can be attached to the grooming arm on the table, which will help keep him secure. Most tables also have non-skid pads on the surface to keep the dog from sliding around. A grooming table will also save your back because it can be adjusted to your height and prevent you from having to bend over or kneel down.

Introduce the grooming table slowly. Place the pup on the table a few times without doing any grooming, but do offer a treat. After you do this a few times, your puppy should eagerly get up on the table. Then you can start lightly brushing him and running any appliances like hair dryers or clippers before actually doing any major grooming. When the dog seems totally comfortable, you can start grooming on a regular basis. This gradual introduction will ensure that your puppy grows to enjoy grooming time with you.

BRUSHING

Brushing your puppy on a daily basis will maintain his good appearance, reduce shedding, keep mats to a minimum, and allow you to inspect the coat for any foreign debris or skin problems. It also stimulates your dog's skin and spreads the coat's natural oils, which help keep a coat shiny and the skin healthy. Puppies who are brushed on a routine basis will need to be bathed less often because most of the dirt and debris in the coat will be removed regularly.

Each coat type will require a different amount of brushing. Dogs with short or smooth coats, such as hounds, can be gone over with a grooming glove a few times a week; however, a dog with a long coat will need daily brushing to keep mats away. There are many breed-specific books on the market that will explain exactly how to groom your dog once he's grown into his adult coat.

Most dogs will thoroughly enjoy the time spent being pampered by you every day.

Wire Stripping

Wiry coats, like those of terriers, must be hand-stripped every three to four months, which means pulling out the dead hair. It can be pulled out with your thumb and finger in the direction of growth, or you can use a stripping knife. If done correctly, it should not hurt the dog at all. It does take practice, however, so it may be wise to have a professional groomer who has worked on wiry coats show you how it's done or have the groomer do it for you. However, if you do not plan to show your wire-haired dog, he can be groomed with a clipper.

Bath Time

The trick is to make bath time as fun and rewarding as possible for your puppy. One owner always leaves treats on the sides of the tub and lets his dog eat them while being bathed. Now all he has to say is "Bath time," and the dog jumps right in.

What puppy can resist lounging on his owner's lap while being brushed—it's a canine paradise!

BATHING

Most puppies will require a bath only occasionally. Healthy dogs are pretty good at keeping themselves clean, and regular brushing should keep your puppy's coat in good shape. Some dogs, like the Chesapeake Bay Retriever and the Great Pyrenees, have waterproof coats, and it is best not to bathe them too often because it can strip the natural oils and reduce the coat's ability to repel water. In fact, overbathing your dog can cause dry skin and irritation, which in turn causes excess scratching or infections. But every puppy, at some time or another, will roll in something particularly smelly or dirty and require a bath.

Bathing Your Puppy

To bathe your puppy:

1. Brush out your puppy's coat and remove all mats.
2. Plug his ears with cotton balls.
3. Place a non-slip rubber mat on the floor of the tub, sink, or plastic bathtub.
4. Soak the coat thoroughly with warm water.
5. Using canine shampoo, and avoiding the head, work up a good lather against the natural direction of the coat.

Have plenty of towels available to dry off your pup after his bath.

6. Carefully wash your dog's face with a washcloth, making sure not to get soap in his eyes.

7. Rinse the coat thoroughly until all the soap is out.

8. If you use a canine conditioner, massage and rinse the coat as you did using the shampoo.

9. Squeeze the excess water from the coat and towel dry the dog. Let the dog shake the excess water out of his coat. Remove the cotton balls.

A Word of Warning: Just-bathed puppies will find the dirtiest spot in which to roll around, so it may be wise to keep them inside until totally dry.

If your dog has a long or clipped coat, you may want to use a hair dryer. Remember to always use a hair dryer on a warm or cool setting—never hot. Your pup's skin can easily burn from the high temperature. While drying, brush the hair straight away from the body.

DENTAL CARE

Your new puppy comes with a brand-new set of puppy teeth. Anyone who has ever raised a puppy is abundantly aware of these teeth—he will chew anything, chase your shoelaces, and play with every piece of clothing.

How Dogs' Teeth Develop

Newborn puppies have no teeth. At about four weeks, puppies begin to get their deciduous or baby teeth. They begin eating semi-solid food, play-fighting with their littermates, and learning discipline

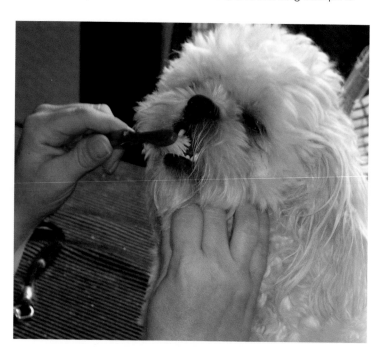

If you do not brush your dog's teeth on a regular basis, plaque builds up on the teeth and under the gums.

Chewing

Puppies need to chew, as it is a necessary part of their physical and mental development. They develop muscles and life skills as they drag objects around and fight over possessions. Puppies chew on things to explore their world and use taste to determine what is food and what is not. Good chew toys can help clean puppy teeth while alleviating the need to chew. Puppies who have adequate chew toys will have less destructive behavior, have better physical development, and have less chance of retaining deciduous teeth. Dogs with good chewing habits as puppies will also have healthier teeth throughout their lives.

from their mother. As their new teeth come in, their mother's feeding sessions become less frequent and shorter. When pups are six to eight weeks of age, the mother will start growling to warn them when they are fighting too roughly or nursing too hard, causing her pain with their new teeth.

At about four months of age, most puppies begin shedding their baby teeth. Often these teeth need some help coming out to make way for the permanent teeth. The incisors (front teeth) will be replaced first, then the adult canine or "fang" teeth. When a baby tooth is not shed and a permanent tooth comes in, veterinarians call it a retained deciduous tooth. This can cause gum infections by trapping hair and debris between the permanent tooth and the retained baby tooth.

By the time dogs reach four years of age, 75 percent have periodontal disease. It is the most common infection in dogs. Yearly examinations by your veterinarian are essential to maintaining healthy teeth. If periodontal disease is detected,

your veterinarian may recommend a prophylactic cleaning. To do a thorough cleaning, it will be necessary to put your dog under anesthesia. Your veterinarian will scale the teeth with an ultrasound scaler or hand instrument, removing the calculus. If the periodontal disease is advanced, the veterinarian may prescribe a medicated mouth rinse or antibiotics for use at home.

As your dog ages, professional oral examinations and cleanings should become more frequent. Your senior dog's mouth should be inspected at least once a year, and eventually your vet may recommend visits every six months.

Oral Exam

You should help maintain your dog's oral health. Examine your puppy's mouth at least weekly throughout the first year to make sure there are no sores, foreign objects, tooth problems, etc. Excessive drooling, head shaking, or bad breath are trouble signs, so consult your veterinarian. By six months of age, all of his permanent teeth will be in, and plaque can start to accumulate on the tooth surfaces. This is when your dog needs good dental care to prevent calculus buildup. Regular brushing, along with safe chew toys, are the best ways to take care of your puppy's teeth.

Brushing Your Puppy's Teeth

If you do not brush your dog's teeth on a regular basis, plaque builds up on the teeth and under the gums. If this plaque is not removed, periodontal disease, which is a bacterial infection, can occur. If left untreated, the bacteria can enter the bloodstream and spread to your puppy's vital organs. Other problems, such as mouth abscesses and tooth loss, can develop as well. Puppies who don't receive good dental care can suffer from really bad breath, a feature that does not endear them to humans.

It is much easier to brush your puppy's

Eating Paste

Never use human toothpaste when brushing your puppy's teeth. Dogs will not spit out the toothpaste like humans do but will swallow it. This can cause stomach upset and other digestive problems. Also, the minty taste that humans enjoy probably will not be as appealing to your puppy as it is to you. Canine toothpaste comes in "doggy-friendly" flavors, such as beef and poultry, which are edible.

teeth than you may think, as long as you have the right supplies. You should purchase a dog toothbrush or a finger toothbrush (a rubber cap that fits over your index finger) and toothpaste made for dogs. Start by getting your puppy used to having your fingers in his mouth. When you are performing the daily once-over, be sure to look in the pup's mouth and lift the lips or flews to expose the gums. Touch the teeth. Soon this will become just another part of your grooming routine. Then put some doggy-flavored toothpaste on the toothbrush and gently rub a few teeth at a time. Be sure to brush the teeth at the gum line.

Use a circular motion when brushing and slowly make your way around your dog's upper teeth. Make sure to get the teeth in the back of the mouth because these are the ones most prone to periodontal disease. When you are finished with the top, do the bottom in the same manner. Daily brushing would be ideal, but try to do it at least four times a week. This will keep your dog's teeth healthy for a long time.

EAR CARE

Do not neglect your puppy's ears when you groom him. Ear infections can be caused by excessive dirt, moisture, and bacteria that accumulate in the ear canal. Dogs with long, floppy ears, like some hounds, retrievers, and spaniels, are especially prone to ear problems because their ear shape prevents good air circulation. Also, dogs who often swim in natural water like lakes or rivers can get bacteria caught in their ears, causing an infection. You must be extremely diligent about keeping ears clean if you have this type of puppy.

Some breeds, like Shih Tzu, Poodles, and Lhasa Apsos, accumulate hair in the ear canal, which can trap dampness and cause infection as well. When taking care of your puppy's ears, the first thing you should do is pluck or trim (with blunt-nosed scissors) the excess hair. To keep them clean, use a cotton ball or washcloth dampened with commercial ear cleaner or mineral oil, and wipe the inside of the earflap. If the ear is sore, has excess wax, or has a bad smell, your pup probably has an ear infection and needs to see the veterinarian immediately.

Dogs with long, floppy ears are prone to ear problems.

Ear Cleaning

Never stick anything into your puppy's ear canal. When cleaning, wipe the outside area of the earflap only, or you may damage his eardrum.

EYE CARE

It is fairly easy to keep your puppy's eyes clear, sparkling, and bright. First, make sure that you keep all debris, including hair, out of the eyes. If you have a breed with a lot of facial hair, like an Old English Sheepdog, Shih Tzu, or Yorkshire Terrier, tie the hair on the top of the head with a rubber band or clip, or if you do not plan to show your dog, keep it trimmed. Wipe your dog's eyes on a regular basis with a cotton ball or washcloth dipped in warm water. If you have a breed with a lot of facial skin folds, like a Bulldog or a Chinese Shar-Pei, be sure to clean within the folds as well. If your puppy's eyes appear red, cloudy, swollen, or have excess tearing, contact your veterinarian.

NAIL AND FOOT CARE

Your puppy's feet really take a beating. They endure the pounding of all that puppy energy and traverse the terrain of every place he explores—over rocks, cement, wood, snow, or grass, your pup's feet get there first and suffer the hardest.

Foot Exam

Always examine your puppy's feet as part of his daily grooming routine. Inspect them after each outing and check that there are no sharp objects, burrs, thorns, seeds, or splinters in the pads or between the toes. If you find anything, remove it gently with a pair of tweezers. Also watch for soreness or blisters. If your puppy shows any signs of soreness or favors one leg, go to the veterinarian immediately.

Hair Trimming

Keep the hair on your dog's feet trimmed because it often hides dirt, fleas, and mites. Use your blunt-nosed scissors to carefully trim the hair as close to the pads as possible. It will also give your dog a cleaner, neater appearance, especially if he has a medium or long coat.

Trimming Your Puppy's Nails

Nail trimming is something that your dog should get used to during puppyhood. The earlier your puppy gets used to nail trimming, the easier and more relaxed grooming time will be for the both of you. Nail trimming is not only for appearances, but it is necessary for your puppy's health and comfort. It can be very difficult to get your puppy to sit still for this, which is why it is recommended to start while he is young. Also, if your puppy has a scary or painful experience, you may not get a second chance, so try to make this procedure as comfortable and routine as possible.

Trimming your puppy's nails is not as hard as it may seem. The easiest way to do it is with a pair of canine nail clippers. You can also use an electric nail grinder

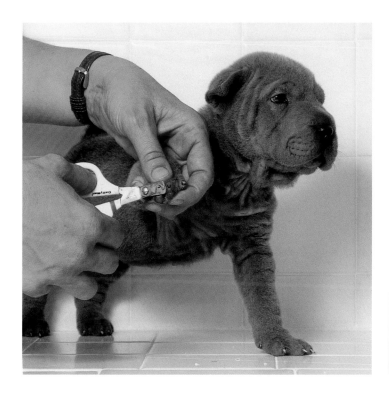

Nail trimming is something that your dog should get used to during puppyhood.

if you find this method easier. Take care to avoid the quick, which is the area of the nail that contains nerves and blood vessels. If you accidentally cut the quick, it will bleed and be painful for your dog.

If your dog has clear or white nails, it is fairly easy to see the quick, which looks like a pink line that extends from the base of the nail toward the tip. If your dog has dark or black nails, it is harder to see where the quick ends.

The best way to trim your puppy's nails is to be conservative and only snip a tiny amount at a time. If you do cut the quick, have a styptic pencil or powder on hand to curb the bleeding.

If it makes you too nervous to trim your puppy's nails—don't ignore the task. Go to an experienced groomer. But if you start now and add it to your weekly schedule, you and your puppy will be nail-trimming experts in no time.

PART THREE

TRAINING

YOUR PUPPY

11

DEVELOPMENT
AND
SOCIALIZATION

Canine behavior is both inherited and learned. Related breeds show tendencies toward certain behavioral characteristics. An experienced breeder should inform you of both the upside and the downside of the breed's personality. Unfortunately, some breeds are labeled with poor temperaments when actually only a small percentage of individuals in the breed have a problem. If there are good temperaments in the background of the pup you have chosen, there is an excellent chance that he will have a good temperament as well. Many temperament or behavior problems are simply due to lack of training or socialization.

Many of us do not realize that our dogs make amazing sacrifices to fit in with human society. In many cases, we tend to forget that dogs are just that—dogs, not human beings. The more you learn about canine behavior, the better you can understand the motivation behind some of your puppy's actions. Once you understand the motivation, it will be easier to correct unwanted behavior and mold your pup into an asset to your family and society in general.

HOW PUPPIES DEVELOP

Most development occurs during the first year of life, which is why it is so important to get on the right track from birth. If not provided with the proper socialization, nutrition, health care, training, and affection during this first year, dogs will have a hard time fitting in with their human family—or society in general.

The Newborn Puppy

For the first three weeks of a puppy's life, the only being of any significance is his mother. She is the source of food,

For the first three weeks of a puppy's life, the only being of any significance is his mother.

warmth, and security. Like a newborn baby, the newborn puppy doesn't do much of anything except eat, sleep, and eliminate.

At four weeks of age, the puppy's littermates are becoming more important. Brothers and sisters provide warmth and security when mother leaves the nest. The puppies are becoming slightly more aware of their environment, and curiosity is beginning to develop. Although their mother is still taking care of their basic needs, the puppies are starting to learn the scent and feel of their brothers and sisters. During this period, puppies learn to use their hearing to follow sounds and their vision to follow moving objects.

At this time, the puppies' mother begins the discipline process. Some people may try to stop the mother from correcting the puppies, but it is important not to interfere. The discipline doled out now will help each puppy accept training in the future. A mother's discipline at this stage of development also teaches the puppies to accept training and affection.

The breeder should be handling the puppies now to get them used to people. At this age, the puppies can learn the difference between their mother's touch and gentle human handling. A puppy who is denied the opportunity to interact with humans while young will have more trouble during the socialization process, which is discussed later in this chapter.

Five to Eight Weeks

Puppies will develop significantly between five and seven weeks of age, learning to recognize the difference between dogs and people and starting to respond to individual voices. They are playing more with littermates. Through this type of play, puppies are learning quite a bit about the world. They will learn how to play nicely with other dogs because they will surely be told by brothers, sisters, and mother when they are getting out of line. Although it may seem as if the puppies in a litter are fighting or playing too roughly, they are just trying to assert their personalities and discover how to interact with other dogs.

The eighth week is a frightening time for most puppies. This is the first of several periods of fear that they will go through during their early development. Puppies should not be taken from their mother between four and eight weeks of age. Those who go to new homes too early may have lasting behavior problems, such as difficulty dealing with other dogs, trouble accepting rules and discipline, and they may become excessively shy, aggressive, or fearful. For example, if puppies leave the breeder's home during this fear period and are taken to the veterinarian by the new owner, they may fear the vet for life. By leaving an eight-week-old puppy with the breeder, mom, and littermates for one or two more weeks, you can avoid any bad experiences that may form a lasting impression.

Nine to Twelve Weeks

Between the 9th and 12th weeks are the perfect time for puppies to go to their new homes. At this age, they are ready to form permanent relationships. Take advantage of this and spend time with your new puppy; play with the youngster and encourage him to explore his surroundings and to meet new people. During this time, you should begin socializing your pup, which is more than simply introducing him to other people, dogs, noises, and sounds. It is making sure that these things do not frighten your puppy as you introduce them. The period between the 8th and 12th weeks is the most important for your puppy's socialization.

Gentle discipline is also very important during this stage of development. Your puppy needs to learn that there are specific rules that must be followed. Puppies will try to get away with anything and everything because they are testing boundaries. Many people have the tendency to let puppies get away with things because they are so cute and small. However, don't let your pup do anything now that you wouldn't want him to do later.

Thirteen to Sixteen Weeks

From 13 through 16 weeks of age, your puppy will be trying to figure out his routine and how he fits in. By now, your pup should have a good idea of what behaviors can and cannot be tolerated in his new home. Consistency is very important, and everyone in the family should enforce the household rules in the same way. Puppies are pretty intelligent and very aware of their surroundings and the dynamics that make up their family. If there is a weak link in the chain of command, your puppy will take

The period between the eighth and twelfth weeks is the most important for your puppy's socialization.

advantage of it. As with children, a puppy will behave for Mom and not for Dad, or vice versa. Some puppies will treat children just like littermates and may start mounting behavior with small children or may nip and wrestle with them. It is your job to prevent this behavior, but make sure you do it in a positive, non-threatening way.

Four to Six Months

Between four and six months of age, protective instincts will develop. If your pup begins to show protectiveness or aggression by growling, snarling, barking, or raising hackles, interrupt this behavior by distracting the dog and giving a basic obedience command that your pup knows well. If you encourage the behavior or correct it harshly, you will be placing too much emphasis on it. For some pups, any attention is good attention, even being scolded for misbehaving. Instead, remain calm and remind him that you are in charge.

Sometime between 17 and 26 weeks many puppies will go through another fear period, and everyday things may suddenly become frightening. Do not reinforce or encourage any of these fears by babying the youngster. Act exactly as you did when the dog was eight weeks old, and things will soon be back to normal.

The Terrible Teens

The teenage experience for a dog is very similar to that of a human adolescent's experience. A dog's teenage stage usually hits at about 12 months of age, although it's not unusual to see it develop

a month or two earlier. You'll know when it happens. One day you will ask your previously well-trained, sweet little puppy to do something he knows very well, such as sit, and your dog will look at you as if he's never heard that word before.

Do you remember your own behavior during adolescence? Basically, it was

> Between four and six months of age, protective instincts will develop.

impossible to believe that anyone could be more embarrassing than your parents. (It's amazing how smart they become once you are a little older!) It's this same attitude that affects teenage dogs. Teenagers (dogs and humans) are constantly striving to prove that they can take care of themselves. They want to be independent, yet they know that they still need the security of their parents' guidance. These conflicting needs seem to drive some teens (and their parents) crazy.

Similar to human teenagers, adolescent puppies push the boundaries of their rules and test their parents' limits. Many dogs at this age act as if they are entirely too cool to listen to you or to hang out with you. Another common teenage behavior includes a lack of manners. Your previously well-mannered puppy may not be able to talk back to you but may start barking at other dogs, jumping on people, or chasing cars.

During this stage of development, you will need to consistently enforce household rules. Hopefully, you and your dog will have already graduated from puppy kindergarten training because that basic control will help. If you haven't started training by this point, now is the time to do so.

Punishment

Do not physically punish your puppy for bad behavior. Prevent him from repeating the infraction and teach an alternate behavior.

Don't allow any behaviors that you would normally not tolerate. You can also institute a "Nothing in Life Is Free" policy, where your juvenile needs to earn everything he gets from you. This would include sitting for petting or treats, sitting before going out the door, and sitting to put on his collar and leash. These exercises help reinforce the rules.

Most importantly, don't take it personally—this rebellion is not aimed at you. It is a very natural part of growing up,

This "play bow" indicates that your puppy is ready for some fun!

and it will pass in a few months, thankfully much quicker in dogs than in humans. Your puppy will eventually mature, and if you are consistent in training, the pup will turn back into that enjoyable friend you once had.

UNDERSTANDING YOUR DOG'S LANGUAGE

Before you start socializing your puppy, there's one other thing you should undertand, and that's how to read your dog's body language.

Dogs cannot talk—and most dog owners often wonder what they might say if they could. Unfortunately, this obstacle can sometimes make it difficult for both parties to get their points across. It's hard for the puppy to understand what the owner wants, and it's hard for the owner to know what the puppy can understand.

Dogs communicate through body language, not only within the pack but with outsiders as well. They also put in a lot of effort to try to understand the things we teach them. The least you can do is try to understand what your pup is telling you. If you can read your puppy's body language, it will be easier for you to communicate with him.

Your puppy will also display different postures that have very specific meanings in the canine world. If you are aware of these postures, you can tell exactly how your dog is feeling.

- **Aggressive:** Ears forward at first, out and down as he escalates, back when attacking; eyes fixed, staring at target; lips raised, mouth slightly open; nose wrinkled; head high; hair raised over rump and back of neck; leaning forward, weight shifted to front; body stiff and tense; front leg may point at target; tail stiff and high over back; lip may quiver; may growl, snarl, and bark
- **Attentive:** Ears up; eyes moving; lips relaxed; head up; hair down; weight equally distributed; tail stiff, horizontal, and moving slowly; no verbal communication
- **Fearful:** Ears back and down; eyes wide opened and fixed; mouth open slightly; head down; hair raised over neck; leaning back, weight shifted to rear; tail tucked tight under abdomen; may tremble and defecate; makes fast moves if threatened; looks for an escape route; whines
- **Passively Submissive:** Ears down; eyes down; lips down; hair down; head down; lying on side or back; tail tucked close to body; may urinate
- **Playful:** Ears up; eyes moving; lips relaxed; hair down; leaning back, weight shifted to rear; front foot may wave at target; tail wagging high, broad, and fast; animated, exaggerated, bouncing movements; may bark, pant, or whine
- **Submissive:** Ears down; eyes down; lips down, retracted horizontally; head down; hair down; leaning back, weight shifted to rear; tail may wag horizontally, hang down, or be tucked close to body; may whine

Classifications of Canine Posture (Tuskegee University, 1993)

PUPPY SOCIALIZATION

Socializing your puppy figures into every aspect of his care and training. What exactly is socialization? In terms of puppy raising, socialization refers to the process of introducing your pet to the surrounding environment and life among people. A puppy cannot recognize or feel comfortable around unfamiliar people or situations. A puppy who has the opportunity to meet all kinds of people—people of different ages, sizes, shapes, and races—will be less likely to be afraid or aggressive toward them. For example, a puppy who has never met an elderly person might shy away from one later in life. Dogs should also meet as many different types of animals as possible. If your puppy learns to tolerate the neighborhood cat without too much fuss, he will be less likely to chase it.

Socialization should include an introduction to everything that is part of your world—water, trees, plants, loud noises, vacuum cleaners, stairs, toys—everything! The more things your pup experiences pleasantly, the less he will be afraid of later.

The Importance of Socialization

Socialization will give your puppy the skills to cope with the world. When dogs are isolated from people at an early age, especially during the all-important first 8 to 12 weeks of life, they will never be able to form a strong attachment to people. Instead of feeling like part of the human pack, they will feel threatened and aggressive toward anyone who approaches.

A puppy can inherit a bad temperament from one or both parents and will consequently not make a good pet or working dog. However, bad temperament can also be caused by a lack of socialization or mistreatment.

How to Socialize Your Puppy

The first step in getting a stable, well-adjusted companion is obtaining a happy puppy from a breeder who is determined to produce dogs with good temperaments. Such a person has taken all the necessary steps to provide early socialization. The puppies should be kept in an environment where they are able to see and be around people, and they should be handled regularly. If your breeder has children, even better—this gives the puppies a chance to meet gentle children in the first weeks of life.

Socializing with humans is critical up through 12 weeks of age. If puppies are not socialized with people by then, they will be timid in later life. As I've mentioned, a puppy should stay with his dam and littermates until at least seven or eight weeks of age because the interaction with siblings will help when meeting other dogs.

Once you bring your puppy home, continue the socialization started by the breeder. You should introduce your puppy to everyone you can. If you have young ones in your family, teach them to treat the puppy with respect. If you do not, find some gentle children to play with your puppy. Introduce the pup to everyone in the neighborhood— the mail carrier, the police officer, the gas station attendant, an elderly neighbor, and anyone else who may come knocking on your door.

Practice teaching your puppy good manners while you make introductions. Now is a good time for him to practice sitting for attention and for you to control barking or jumping up. Let each person give a treat (that you provide) when your puppy behaves. After a while, your pup will be thrilled to meet anyone you care to introduce.

You should also visit as many different places as you can—the beach, the park, and the store. Expose your pup to different noises and situations, such as busy streets or crowded pet supply stores—always on leash, of course. However, while this kind of socialization is important, so is your puppy's health. Until he has completed his vaccinations for parvo and distemper, don't let him walk on grass in public parks, rest stops,

Teach children to treat your puppy with respect.

new things at once. Socialization should take place gradually.

- Don't force your puppy to approach things that he is afraid of, as it will only make the situation worse.
- If he is frightened of something, don't reinforce fears by coddling or encouraging him to be frightened in any way.
- Don't let people overstimulate the puppy. (Children are especially guilty of this.) Make sure you supervise the pup around new people and give plenty of "down" time for puppy relaxation.
- Don't let people surprise your puppy or handle him too often. A pup should explore the environment at his own pace.
- Don't socialize your puppy without vaccinations.

or other places that unimmunized dogs may have pottied. Carry your puppy in your arms instead. When you go places where you know only well-cared-for dogs hang out (such as a responsible friend's home), put your puppy on the ground and let him explore!

Introduce him to other well-socialized dogs; puppies must learn to get along with other dogs as well as with humans. Find a puppy kindergarten class in your area and attend regularly. Not only is it a great place to socialize your dog, it is also the first step in training the new addition to your family.

Socialization Don'ts

Here's a few things to avoid when socializing your puppy:

- Don't overwhelm your puppy with lots of

STARTING OVER

Perhaps you have taken home an older puppy or adult dog from a shelter, and you do not have firsthand knowledge of his previous socialization. Perhaps you already know that the puppy has been mistreated or neglected when very young. All is not lost; there are plenty of things that you can do to get your puppy on the right track.

First, you need to inquire about the puppy's social experience and find out as much as you can about his early weeks of life. Kennel dogs may have a difficult time adjusting to people and environmental stimuli. Some puppies have been mistreated, and this fear or resentment will linger. For example, if your puppy was mistreated by a woman, he may prefer men. Some dogs may hold a

grudge against everyone in uniform. Perhaps your puppy is afraid of water, the car, or loud sirens. These fears can probably all be traced back to a traumatic experience in the formative weeks of life.

Once your puppy has been vaccinated, introduce him to other well-socialized dogs.

You need to approach these problems very gradually and carefully, especially if your dog is aggressive toward people. Do not throw your puppy at the very thing that is frightening; that will only make the situation worse. Introduce kind, gentle people to your puppy slowly and in small increments. For example, if your puppy is afraid of the mail carrier, take him out on lead when the mail is delivered. With the mail carrier's permission, of course, be reassuring and have your pup sit when the carrier approaches. Act perfectly normal toward the person, carry on a brief conversation, and then have the mail carrier give your puppy a treat. Do this over a period of weeks. By now, your pup should at least be able to control these fears and not act shyly or aggressively. Do the same for any frightening situation.

Basic training is also very helpful. Performing commands gives your puppy something to concentrate on other than what's causing his fear. Plus, it helps him concentrate on you. This should be reassuring and make your dog feel more comfortable in any situation.

Your puppy may never get over some fears entirely, but with careful conditioning and training, he should be able to cope with daily activities without problems. If your puppy is not responding and is still acting aggressively, you should consult an experienced trainer for professional advice.

12

CRATE TRAINING AND HOUSETRAINING

When you first bring your dog home, you will probably be given plenty of advice from friends and neighbors who own dogs. You will also undoubtedly read lots of articles and books on how to raise and train your dog. No matter what anyone tells you, there is really no one training method that is superior to all others—as there is no one dog who is exactly like another. Each puppy is an individual and will respond to different techniques.

However, a dog never becomes disobedient, unruly, or a menace to society without the full consent of his owner. Through heredity, genetics, or environment, your puppy may have certain limitations, but in most instances, the single biggest limitation is the owner's inability to understand the dog's needs and how to cope with them.

There is no breed that cannot be trained. Granted, there are some dogs who provide their owners with real challenges, but in most cases, these problems have more to do with the trainer than the dog. It is often simply a matter of taking the time to find out what truly motivates your puppy. Once you find a motivator, your dog will be more than willing to learn. In order to develop your puppy's potential, you should begin training the moment you bring him home.

Your eight- to ten-week-old puppy is not too young to learn; in fact, this knowledge will help your dog better deal with his new surroundings. After leaving the comfort of their mother and littermates, puppies will be insecure and look to you for direction.

Time-Out

Sometimes puppies really just need to get away from it all. The hustle and bustle of a busy household can be overwhelming at times. There are times when your puppy will get overstimulated and need to take a "time-out" to calm down (especially if you have rambunctious kids around). A crate is great for all of these times, and it should be used as your puppy's place of refuge. Soon the puppy will think it is pretty cool, too.

When you establish rules from the start, you can prevent bad habits that you'll only end up dealing with later.

CRATE TRAINING

By about five weeks of age, most puppies are starting to move away from their mom and littermates to relieve themselves. This instinct to keep the bed clean is the basis of crate training. Crates work well because puppies don't want to soil where they eat and sleep. They also like to curl up in small dark places that offer protection on three sides because it makes them feel more secure.

Being confined in the crate will help a puppy develop better bowel and bladder control. When confined for gradually lengthened periods of time, the dog will learn to avoid soiling his bed. It is your responsibility to give your pup plenty of time outside the crate and the house, or the training process will not be successful.

Crate training helps your puppy feel comfortable and secure in his crate. This can provide a number of benefits for the dog owner, who may then be able to use the crate to assist with housetraining or for confinement when traveling or showing. Formerly den animals, dogs can learn to tolerate and even enjoy spending time in a crate, especially if they are acclimated to a crate at a young age.

Crate Size

When choosing a crate, it is important to get the right size. The crate should be just large enough for an adult dog to stand and turn around comfortably. Unless you plan to purchase two crates—one for your puppy now and one when he's fully grown—this means purchasing a crate that's bound to be too large for your puppy. Although dogs generally do not like to soil the place where they sleep, getting a crate that is too large may result in the puppy using a portion of it to potty. To prevent this, block off the back half of it with a crate divider to decrease the size until he's an adult.

How Long Should You Crate Your Puppy?

Crates can be misused. They are not a means of ignoring your pup, nor are they meant to become a place of isolation or loneliness. Young puppies should not spend more than four hours at a time in a crate and should always be given plenty of time outdoors and with the family.

Perhaps the biggest misuse of crates

is to use them to confine a dog for long periods while the owners are at work. Only use the crate for short-term confinement, no more than a few hours at a time. Keeping a dog confined to such a small space for long periods is not good for a dog's physical and emotional health. For longer periods of confinement, it is best to use a puppy pen or small room.

Crate Location

During the day, keep your puppy's crate in a location that allows easy access and permits him to be part of the family. The laundry room or backyard will make a puppy feel isolated and unhappy, especially if he can hear people walking around. Place it anywhere the family usually congregates—the kitchen or family room is often the best.

At night, especially when your puppy is still getting used to the crate, the ideal place is in your bedroom, near your bed. Having you nearby will create a feeling of security and will be easier for you as well. If your puppy needs to go outside during the night, you can let him out before he has an accident. Your pup will also be comforted by the smell, sight,

General Guidelines

AGE OF PUPPY	MAXIMUM LENGTH OF TIME FOR CRATING
8–12 weeks	Up to 1 hour
12–16 weeks	Up to 3 hours
16–24 weeks	Up to 5 hours
24 weeks and up	Up to 6 hours

and sound of you and will be less likely to feel frightened.

How to Crate Train

To begin crate training, place the crate in a prominent location in your home, and leave the door open so that your puppy can explore it if he wants. The crate should have some form of soft bedding inside, such as a blanket or fleece liner. If your puppy is not showing any fear of the crate, start putting treats just outside the crate door and eventually inside the door to encourage him to put his head inside. Gradually place the treats farther inside the crate to convince

During the day, keep your puppy's crate in a location that permits him to be part of the family.

him to enter it. Do not try to push your puppy too fast during this process, or you may make him fearful.

When your puppy is comfortable entering the crate to retrieve a treat, practice putting some of his favorite toys inside the crate for him to retrieve. Throughout the crate training process, you should encourage your puppy to explore, play, and sleep in his crate so that he can learn that it is his personal territory. When he seems confident about entering and exiting the crate on his own, attempt to feed him in it by placing his food dish just inside the entrance. Again, gradually move the food farther into the crate until your puppy is eating his meals inside. When you have reached this stage, you can begin to close the crate

Crate Don'ts

- Don't let your puppy out of the crate when crying or scratching at the door. If you do, the dog will think that complaining will bring release every time. The best thing to do for a temper tantrum is to ignore the pup. Only open the door when he is quiet and has calmed down.

- Don't use the crate as punishment. If you use the crate when your dog does something bad, he will think of the crate as a bad place. Even if you want to get your dog out of the way, make sure that you offer lots of praise for going into the crate and give him a treat or toy, too.

door while your puppy is eating and then open it immediately when he is done.

The next stage of crate training involves conditioning your puppy to spend longer periods in the crate. Always make sure your puppy has had a potty break prior to crating him, and then put him in his crate for 10 or 15 minutes while you are at home. These crating sessions can become successively longer if your puppy is tolerating them well. Treating and praising your puppy when he enters the crate willingly encourages him to cooperate. If you give your dog the command to "kennel," and give him a treat while he is entering the crate willingly, he will soon learn to enter his crate on command.

The next step is to crate your puppy for short periods of time when you leave the house. Tell your puppy to kennel, and reward him when he does. You should not fuss over your puppy prior to leaving or upon your return. Keep departures and arrivals as subdued as possible. Putting a chew toy or treat-releasing toy in the crate will help keep your puppy busy and comfortable while you are gone.

You should continue to crate your puppy occasionally when you are home so that he does not associate crate confinement with you leaving him alone.

Do not crate your puppy for more than two to four hours at a time, depending on his age and stage of bladder control. You do not want him to get in the habit of eliminating in his crate. When not in use, leave the crate open for your puppy to use at will. He will begin to accept the crate as his safe refuge and not something to be dreaded.

HOUSETRAINING

One of the first things that you will undertake after acquiring your puppy will be housetraining him. You are teaching your dog that there is a specific place to eliminate, preferably outside. Your best bet is to start housetraining as soon as possible. However, you need to remember that puppies between the ages of 8 and 16 weeks will not have control of their bladders or bowels. They will not be able to "hold it" until they get a little older, which means that in the beginning, housetraining will take vigilance on your part.

Puppies usually have to go to the bathroom after eating, drinking, sleeping, and playing. You will have to watch very carefully for signs that your puppy needs to eliminate, like circling or sniffing the floor. These behaviors are a sure sign that your puppy needs to go outside. When you see them, don't hesitate to carry your pup outside to the spot you have chosen for his elimination. Give lots of praise when he goes potty in the right place.

Most puppies have a bad habit of thinking it's time to play when they get outside, and they forget about going to the bathroom. If you start the

Give lots of praise when your puppy eliminates in the right place.

housetraining process early enough, you can teach your puppy to potty on command. When you take him outside, use a command for eliminating, such as "potty time," "hurry up," or "do your business." Use any command you are comfortable with and use it every time that you take your puppy to the bathroom spot. Soon, he will learn the command and go when you say it.

With the help of a regular schedule, you will be able to predict the times that your puppy will need to potty. The most useful thing that you can buy for him is a crate. Training your puppy to use the crate is the quickest and easiest way to housetrain him. Remember that your puppy will be developing habits that will last a lifetime—make sure that you teach him the right ones.

Establish a Schedule

Puppies need time to develop bowel and bladder control. The best way to most accurately predict when your puppy needs to eliminate is to establish a routine that works well for both of you and stick to it. If you make a daily schedule of eating, drinking, and outside time and follow it, you will see your puppy progress.

Every person and family will have a different routine—there is no one right schedule for everyone. Just make sure that you arrange times and duties that everyone can stick with. The schedule you set up will have to work with your normal routine and lifestyle. Your first priority in the morning will be to get the puppy outdoors. Just how early this will take place will depend much more on

your puppy than on you. Once your puppy comes to expect a morning walk, there will be no doubt in your mind when he needs to go out. You will also very quickly learn to tell a puppy's "emergency" signals. Do not test the young puppy's ability for self-control. A vocal demand to be let out is confirmation that the housetraining lesson is learned.

Puppies usually learn very quickly how to get your attention to go out. Unfortunately, they may learn some bad habits in the process—like barking, whining, jumping on you, or scratching at your door. You can redirect this behavior and teach your puppy a positive way to get your attention, such as ringing a bell to go outside. Hang a cowbell on the back door and smear it with some kind of treat—a little cheese works well. Each time you take your puppy outside to potty, have him reach up to lick off the cheese, thereby ringing the bell. Also ring the bell every time you let your puppy out. The action of going out is now associated with the sound of the bell and the treat. After a few months, your dog should get the picture and start ringing the bell to go outside.

It is also important to limit your puppy's freedom inside the house and keep a watchful eye on him at all times. Many puppies won't take the time to go outside to relieve themselves because they are

afraid they will miss something; after all, everything exciting happens in the house. That's where all the family members usually are. Unfortunately, you may find your puppy sneaking off somewhere—behind the sofa or to another room—to relieve himself. By limiting the puppy's freedom, you can prevent some of these mistakes. Close bedroom doors and put baby gates across hallways. If you can't supervise the pup, consider the crate.

One way to constantly supervise your puppy is to use what some trainers call the "puppy umbilical cord." Start by attaching one end of a long leash to your puppy's collar and the other end to you. Now everywhere that you go, your dog goes, and vice versa. This method will help prevent accidents because you'll be much quicker to notice any signs that your puppy has to go outside.

Sample Schedule

The following is an example of a schedule that might work for you and your family, although remember that any schedule can work as long as you can give your dog the necessary attention.

- 7:00 am—Take the puppy outside. (This time might be even earlier for young puppies who have a hard time holding it all night.) After the puppy goes potty, give him lots of praise and bring

him back inside. Fix the puppy's breakfast, offer water, and then take him out in the backyard.

> The best way to housetrain your puppy is to establish a routine that works well for both of you and stick to it.

- 8:00 am—Go outside to play with the puppy for a few minutes before leaving for the day. Just before you leave, put him inside the crate and give him a treat and a toy.
- 12:00 pm—If at all possible, come home for lunch, let your puppy out of the crate, and bring him outside to eliminate. If you or another family member can't do it, try to find a neighbor (a retired person or stay-at-home parent might be a good idea) or hire a dog walker to come over. Take this time to exercise and play with your puppy.
- 3:00 pm—If you have school-age children, make sure one of them comes straight home from school to take the puppy outside, walk, and play with him for a while. After playing, let the puppy hang out while your child does homework or watches television. If you do not have kids, you may be able to pay a teenager in your neighborhood to come over after school.
- 6:00 pm—If you are just arriving home and your dog has been confined for a few hours, immediately let him outside to eliminate and play. Feed the puppy after you eat dinner and take him outside to potty.

- 8:00 pm—After some quality family time, puppy included, do a little bit of grooming, offer some water, and then take the pup outside to eliminate.
- 11:00 pm—Take the puppy outside one last time before going to bed.

Keep in mind that he should not remain in the crate for longer than three to four hours at a time, except during the night. In addition, the puppy will need to go out after waking up, eating, playtime, and every three to four hours in between.

When housetraining your puppy, don't let success go to your head. A few weeks without a mistake does not mean that your puppy is completely housetrained, but it does mean your routine is working. Stick to the schedule for as long as possible. A regular schedule will be helpful now and throughout your dog's lifetime.

Accidents Will Happen

When housetraining your dog, remember that if the puppy has an accident, it means that he was not supervised well enough or wasn't taken outside in time. If you catch your dog in the act, don't yell or scold him. Simply say, "No!" loudly, which should startle and stop the dog. Pick him up and go outside so that he can continue eliminating in the regular relief area. Praise the pup for finishing outside. If you scold or punish him, you are teaching him that you think going potty is wrong. Your dog will become sneaky about it, and you will find puddles and piles in strange places. Don't punish; emphasize the praise for eliminating in the right place.

If your puppy does eliminate in your house, make sure you clean it up right away with a pet-odor neutralizer, which can be bought in a pet store. This should keep him from using the same spot again. You can also scrub the area thoroughly with a solution of 1/4 cup of white vinegar and a squirt of liquid detergent mixed with 1 quart of warm water.

Housetraining is one of the most important gifts we can give our dogs. It allows them to live as one of the family. Every puppy will make mistakes, especially in the beginning. Do not worry—with the proper training and lots of patience, every dog can be housetrained.

Don't punish your dog for housetraining accidents.

13

BASIC TRAINING FOR GOOD BEHAVIOR

All puppies not only need basic training—they deserve it. Dogs do not automatically know how they should behave, so they need rules to follow. Puppies' rights include having the basic tools in order to fit in with the new family. Once dogs know these things, they are usually perfectly willing to do whatever is necessary in order to fit in with the family. When you provide this opportunity, you are ensuring that you and your puppy will get along beautifully for the duration of your life together.

WHY IS TRAINING IMPORTANT?

When you added a puppy to your family, you probably wanted a companion and a friend. You may have wanted a dog to accompany you on walks, jog alongside you, or play with your children. Perhaps you wanted to get involved in dog sports or events. To do any of these things, your puppy will need training.

Training is important because it will transform your jumpy, squirmy, wiggly little puppy into a well-mannered dog who is a joy to be around. A trained puppy won't jump up on people, dash out the door, or raid the trash can.

All puppies need to have someone tell them what to do. Puppies have the right to be trained—it is unfair to expect them to figure out the human world on their own, and they won't be able to do it.

You, too, will benefit from training, because you will learn how to motivate your puppy, how to prevent problem behaviors, and how to correct mistakes that do happen. Puppy training entails much more than the traditional *sit, down, stay*, and *come* commands—it means that you will be teaching your puppy how to live in your house. You can set some rules and expect him to follow them.

First, you must decide exactly what you want training to accomplish. You probably want your puppy to be calm and well behaved around people and well mannered when out in public. Maybe you would like to participate in dog activities and sports. The things that you can do with your puppy are unlimited. Decide

Household Rules

When establishing household rules, picture your pup as an adult. It may be cute to let your cuddly Saint Bernard puppy sit on your lap while you watch TV, but are you going to want a 150-pound (68-kg) lapdog a year from now? It may be hilarious to watch your little Chihuahua valiantly defend toys by growling at you, but in a few months the growling may turn into snapping if you don't curb this aggressiveness. Take a practical look at your life, your puppy, and your environment, and decide what behavior you can and cannot live with. It is important to make this decision now, early in your puppy's life, rather than later, because what your dog learns as a pup, he will continue doing as an adult.

what you would like to do and then embark on a training program to achieve those goals.

PRINCIPLES OF POSITIVE TRAINING

Your goal right from the start in training should be to forge a bond of trust, mutual respect, and understanding with your puppy. If you also teach him that learning is fun, training at all levels will progress more quickly and you and your puppy will enjoy each other more. The most effective and fair way to forge such a bond is through positive reinforcement.

Positive reinforcement is the process of rewarding your puppy for doing what you want him to do. The reward has to be something that your pup likes and wants—for many dogs, food is highly motivating, but toys, petting, and even a chance to run in circles can all be rewards if the individual dog is motivated to work for them. It's your job to figure out what really motivates your individual dog.

Four main components are used to shape a dog's behavior: rewards, consequences, repetition, and consistency. A training program that lacks any one of these components is not a comprehensive training program and will suffer in its effectiveness. Certain training practices also can enhance communication, produce better results, and make training an enjoyable activity for both dogs and their owners.

Rewards

Rewards, of course, exist to encourage appropriate behavior, and they can consist of treats, favorite toys, petting, praise, or

Most puppies respond to food as a reward, but some may prefer play or toys.

playtime. For rewards to be effective, you must offer them immediately so that the puppy can associate the reward with his behavior. In the interest of letting the dog know instantaneously when he has displayed the correct behavior, many trainers now use clickers to let the dog know he will be rewarded. This can also be accomplished by saying the word

rap due to their negative nature and the horror of past training methods that employed unnecessarily harsh methods, like jerking on the dog's collar. But even positive training methods must use consequences if they are to be effective. Modern training methods use gentler forms of consequences, such as withholding rewards or attention. And like rewards, consequences must be imposed immediately in order for the dog to associate them with his behavior. This is why punishing a dog after the fact is not effective.

If a behavior has already occurred, as in the case of a dog who gets into trouble when his owner isn't present, it is best to ignore the behavior and take steps to prevent it from happening in the future. Also, never impose consequences if the dog behaves inappropriately while learning a new skill. This only serves to dampen his willingness to learn. Only use consequences when a dog consciously disobeys a learned skill.

"yes" when a dog behaves correctly, followed by offering the promised reward. Praise should

The most effective and fair way to forge a bond with your puppy is through positive reinforcement.

always be delivered in your happiest, most upbeat tone of voice. If treats are used, you should choose a treat that is sufficiently appealing to motivate your puppy but not so alluring that he cannot concentrate on the task at hand.

Consequences

Consequences help discourage inappropriate behavior. However, consequences have received a bad

Repetition

Repetition is required in any learning process. Not only does it facilitate the retention of what is learned, but it also provides practice to improve performance. Learning theorists call this classical conditioning, and indeed, repetition conditions our dogs to behave the way we desire. Puppies require more repetition than adult dogs because their juvenile minds do not have the retention abilities of a mature dog. Even after a skill is learned, occasional repetition keeps a dog's skills in top form.

Consistency

Consistency prevents confusion. For example, if you feed your dog scraps from the dinner table one night and admonish him for begging the following night, the mixed messages you are giving sabotage your attempts to train your dog not to beg. When training is executed in a consistent manner, the dog learns what is expected of him, and he also knows what to expect of you. Consistent communication is a source of security for a dog because most dogs only want to please their humans.

BEFORE YOU TRAIN

Adhering to some basic training principles will prevent breakdowns in communication and help you to achieve your training goals together.

Learn Patience

Patience is not necessarily a requirement of training, but it can certainly make teaching and learning more pleasurable for you and your puppy. If you find yourself losing patience, it is best to stop the training session and try again another time. You should always try to end a training session on a positive note. Ask your dog to perform a simple exercise that he already knows well, reward the dog, and then end the session.

Teach Hand Signals

Hand signals are often used in formal training, in addition to voice commands. Teaching your dog to respond to hand signals can come in handy when working with him from a distance or when noise levels are high. They are also required for advanced obedience training. Hand signals often evolve from the exaggerated hand movements used to manipulate a treat in the process of training, but they become more subtle as a dog learns the skill.

Dogs tend to learn hand signals quite readily. Because they are not capable of a complex spoken language, as humans are, they rely quite heavily on visual cues and are experts at interpreting body language. For this reason, dogs often respond better to hand signals than voice commands, but it is important for your dog to learn to respond to both. If you use hand signals, then you should give the voice command and hand signal separately, not at the same time (preferably, the voice command first). Hands are a wonderful human feature, but they are often quite busy. Thus, when you cannot use your hands to instruct your dog, voice commands are essential.

Hand Signals

People usually think that obeying hand signals is something that only dogs with advanced training can do. Actually, you can start teaching your puppy hand signals from the very beginning. Ask your trainer to help you incorporate hand signals as you learn the commands and use them in your everyday practice. They can be very useful, especially when your dog is at a distance from you.

Basic Obedience Hand Signals

No standard hand signals are used in dog training. Many hand signals evolve naturally during the training process, such as placing a hand on the floor as if placing a treat there to encourage a down. You can develop any kind of hand signal that most closely follows your training technique and is easiest for your dog to associate with a skill.

The following hand signals are the most common signals used in basic obedience training:

- **Come:** Wave your hand toward your body in a "come follow me" motion.
- **Sit:** With your flat palm facing up, raise your arm from the elbow as if lifting a dumbbell, drawing your palm to your chest.
- **Down:** With your palm facing down, make a level, downward motion with your hand.
- **Stay:** With arm outstretched, your flat palm should be facing your dog as if you were stopping traffic.

Establish Eye Contact and Name Recognition

As a method of communication, training is not effective if you do not have your puppy's attention. If you try to talk to someone who is on the phone, reading a book, or watching television, she may only hear a fraction of what you say. Likewise, if your puppy is distracted, you cannot communicate with him effectively. It is important to establish eye contact with your dog before asking him to perform a skill.

Dogs tend to learn hand signals quite readily.

A good way to establish eye contact and teach your puppy to respond to his name at the same time is to reward him every time he looks at you when you say his name. Throughout the day, say your puppy's name frequently, and reward him each time he looks at you. This conditions him to be very responsive to his name. Then, when it is time for training, you can say your puppy's name to get his attention.

Keep Training Sessions Short

Training sessions are most productive when they are short and frequent. If you try to feed your puppy too much training at once, he may become frustrated or bored. At this point, his mind will begin to wander, and any further training will be ineffective. With this in mind, limit training sessions for puppies to ten minutes. (When he's an adult, he will be able to tolerate about 15 to 20 minutes of training at a time.) You can keep your puppy focused during training by varying the skills you are working on so that your dog does not become bored with performing the same task repeatedly.

To get the most value out of your training, sessions should be conducted a minimum of three times per week to provide enough repetition. It also helps to limit the number of new skills you are teaching, because trying to teach too much too fast can result in confusion. Perfect the skills you are working on before moving to something new.

PROFESSIONAL TRAINING

When it comes to training your puppy, one option is to find a trainer to help

Find a trainer who uses postive methods and understands your breed.

you out. If you decide to take your puppy to a training class, you must do your homework. It should be your mission to find the trainer in your area who would be best for both you and your puppy.

Finding an Instructor or Trainer

Referrals are probably the best place to start when trying to find an instructor or trainer. If you have admired a neighbor's well-behaved puppy, ask where he went for training. Call your veterinarian, breeder, or groomer and ask who she recommends. Make notes about each referral. What did people like and dislike about this trainer? You will want an experienced trainer who can handle any situation that may arise. However, experience is not the only qualification. Some people who have been training dogs for years are still using the same teaching methods and haven't learned any new techniques. Ideally, the trainer you choose should be knowledgeable about your dog's breed characteristics, personality, and temperament and know how to train him. If she doesn't like the breed, go elsewhere.

A good training instructor will belong to a professional training organization. The Association of Pet Dog Trainers (APDT) is one of the most prominent groups. The APDT publishes regular newsletters to share information, techniques, and new developments with their members. APDT members are more likely to be up-to-date on training techniques and styles, as well as information about specific dog breeds. To find an APDT instructor in your area, go to www.apdt.com.

Questions to Ask the Trainer

Once you have a list of referrals for dog trainers in your area, call the instructors and ask questions such as:
- How long have you been teaching classes?
- What do you think of my breed?
- Do you use positive training methods?
- Do you belong to any professional organizations?
- Can I observe your classes? There should be no reason why you cannot

attend a class to observe the instructor. (If you can't watch, cross this one off your list.)

When you go to watch the class, ask yourself these questions:
- Would you let this person handle your dog?
- How does the instructor relate to the dogs?
- Are the dogs relaxed and looking like they're having a good time?
- Are the dogs paying attention to the instructor?

If you're still not sure, don't be afraid to keep asking questions. You are paying a trainer to provide a service, and you must be sure that both you and your puppy will be comfortable with your decision.

Puppy Kindergarten

The next step in training should be a class that is geared just for puppies. Puppy kindergarten classes consist of obedience training and socialization and are for puppies between the ages of 10 and 16 weeks. A puppy owner also learns how to prevent problem behaviors from occurring and how to establish household rules. Every puppy can benefit from this type of class. It will teach the foundations of training, as well as provide an excellent opportunity for socialization with other dogs and people. A good puppy kindergarten class will teach you how to train and teach your dog obedience commands like *come, sit, stay, down,* and *heel.* Participating in a kindergarten class with your puppy will strengthen the bond between you, bring you closer together, and help you to learn the right way to train your dog. After your puppy passes puppy kindergarten, the sky's the limit!

BASIC TRAINING

Although your puppy should attend puppy kindergarten, begin training as soon as he is comfortable in your home and knows his name. It is also very helpful to take the lessons that you learn together in kindergarten and practice them at home. Doing your "homework" together will not only reinforce what you learn in class, it will allow you to spend some quality one-on-one time with your pup.

There are two very important things to remember when training your puppy: Train him without any potential distractions and keep all lessons very short. Eliminating any distraction is important because it is essential that you have your pup's full attention. This is not possible if there are other people, other dogs, butterflies, or birds to play with. Also, as we mentioned earlier, puppies have very short attention spans. Even when the pup has become a young adult, the maximum time you should train would be about 20 minutes. However, you can give the puppy more than one lesson a day, three being as many as recommended, each spaced well apart. If you train any longer, the puppy will become bored, and you will end the session on a down note, which you should never do.

Before beginning a lesson, always play a little game so that the puppy is in an active state of mind and more receptive to training. Likewise, always end lessons with play and on a high note, lavishly praising the puppy, which will build his confidence.

Collar and Leash Training

Training a puppy to a collar and leash is easy and something you can start doing at home without assistance. Start with a soft nylon collar. The puppy will initially try to bite at it but will soon forget it's there, more so if you play with him. Some people leave the dog's collar on all of the time, while others put it on only when they are taking the dog out. If it is to be left on, purchase a narrow or round one so that it does not mark the coat or become snagged on furniture.

Once the puppy ignores the collar, you can attach the leash to it and let him pull it behind him for a few minutes every day.

Training a puppy to accept a collar and leash is easy.

However, if the pup starts to chew at the leash, simply keep it slack and let him choose where to go. The idea is to let him get the feel of the leash but not get in the habit of chewing it. Repeat this a couple of times a day for two days, and the pup will get used to the leash without feeling restrained.

Now, you can let the pup understand that the leash will be restrictive. The first time this happens, your dog will either pull, buck, or just sit down. Immediately call the pup to you and give lots of praise. Never tug on the leash or drag the puppy along the floor. This might cause him to associate the leash with negative consequences. After a few lessons, the puppy will be familiar with the restrictive feeling, and you can start going in the opposite direction from him. Start walking away from him, call him to you enthusiastically, and continue walking. When the puppy is walking happily on the leash, end the lesson with lots of praise. There is no rush for your puppy to learn leash training, so take as long as you need to make him feel comfortable.

Watch Me

Have you ever been to a very busy city? Do you remember what it was like to have your senses bombarded for the first time with all the sights, smells, and sounds? Think of your puppy as living there, in that initial overwhelming moment, just about all the time.

Puppies have more acute senses than do people. Because they can smell and hear things that you can't, their environments are very rich. This also explains why they are so easily distracted. It's very normal for a puppy to pay close attention to you one second, then completely forget that you exist the next. Something as simple as a clod of dirt could completely enchant your puppy and capture his attention. This is why it's a good idea to teach him a command for paying attention.

Start with some treats in your hand. Show your puppy a treat, and give him the cue "Watch me." Draw the treat up to your eyes. When he looks you in the eye (he'll really be looking at the treat, but that's okay) say

It's a good idea to teach your puppy a command for paying attention.

"Yes!" and give him the treat. After a couple repetitions, your puppy should be following the treat up to your eyes and looking at your face. At this point, stop holding a treat up to your eyes but continue to use your same hand signal. Draw your empty hand up to your eyes. When he looks you in the eye, say "Yes!" and give him a treat.

When your puppy is looking you in the eyes regularly when you give him the cue, you can gradually wean off the hand signal if you choose.

The *Come* Command

The *come* command (also called the *recall*) is possibly the most important one you can teach—it may even save your pup's life someday. It ensures that your dog will return to you immediately when you call, even if there is any kind of distraction or danger nearby.

Teaching your puppy to come when called should always be a pleasant experience. You should never call your puppy in order to scold or yell at him, or he will soon learn not to respond. When your pup comes to you, make sure to give lots of praise, petting, and in the beginning, a treat. If your dog expects happy things when reaching your side, you'll never have trouble getting him to come to you.

Initially, work with your puppy in the home by calling him occasionally and rewarding him when he comes. Call your puppy from different rooms and at different times of the day, always indicating that he has responded correctly with a "yes" and rewarding him.

Just to Be Near You

Puppyhood is the easiest time to teach the *come* command because most puppies want to be near you anyway. Take advantage of this natural reaction and start teaching the *come* command as soon as you get your puppy home. Whenever he decides to run to you, just give the *come* command. The dog will learn to associate the action with the words.

He will quickly learn that coming when called is in his best interest.

When working outside, practice the *recall* with your puppy on a long line. Let your puppy wander to the length of the line and then call him to you and reward him accordingly. Because the goal is to encourage the puppy to want to obey you, always call him in a cheery voice, and encourage him with claps or other noises.

When your puppy is a little bit older, you can practice off leash in a safely enclosed area. Encourage your puppy to come to you by running away from him while calling his name. This may arouse his desire to chase, and he will come back in your direction.

If you can find an assistant to help you, practice the *recall* by having the assistant hold the puppy on a leash. Find a position some distance away and then call the puppy using verbal encouragement and running away from him. The assistant can release the puppy as he responds to the

recall, and give lots of praise and a treat when your pup gets to you. Only practice

Use a long line when practicing the *come* command outside.

this in a safe, enclosed area in case the puppy becomes distracted.

The *Sit* Command

The *sit* command can be used to gain control of your puppy and give him something to do instead of something you don't want him to do, like jumping on you or spinning in circles while you try to put his leash on. If you plan to compete in obedience or agility, a good *sit* response is essential. As with most basic commands, your puppy will learn this one in just a few lessons.

Get a treat that your dog really likes and hold it right by his nose so that all attention is focused on it. Raise the treat above his head and say "Sit." The puppy will follow the treat and automatically sit. Give him the treat for being such a good dog, and don't forget to praise him. After a while, the pup will begin to associate the word *"Sit"* with the action. Most puppies will catch on very quickly. Once your dog is sitting reliably with the treat, take it away and just use praise as a reward.

When the puppy understands the command and does it right away, you can slowly move backward so that you are a few feet (m) away. If he attempts to come to you, simply go back to the original position and start again. Do not attempt to keep the pup in the *sit* position for too long. Even a few seconds is a long time for an impatient, energetic puppy, and you do not want your dog to get bored with lessons before he even begins them.

The *Stay* Command

The *stay* command should follow the *sit*, but it can be very hard for puppies to understand. Remember that your puppy wants nothing more than to be at your side, so it will be hard for a dog to stay in one place while you walk away. You should only expect your pup to perform this command for a few seconds at first, and gradually work up to longer periods of time.

Face the puppy and say "Sit." Now step backward, saying "Stay." It is also very helpful to use a hand signal for *stay*— place your hand straight out, palm toward the dog's nose. Let the pup remain in the position for only a few seconds before saying, "Come," and giving lots of praise and a treat. Once your dog gets the hang of it, repeat the command again, but step farther back. If the pup gets up and comes to you, simply go back to the original position and start again. As the pup starts to understand the command, you can move farther and farther back.

Once your puppy is staying reliably from a short distance, the next test is to walk away after placing the pup. This will mean that your back is to the dog, which will tempt

The *stay* can be used in the *sit* or *down* position.

him to follow you. Keep an eye over your shoulder, and the minute the pup starts to move, spin around, say "Stay," and start over from the original position.

As the weeks go by, you can increase the length of time the pup is left in the *stay* position—but two to three minutes is quite long enough for a puppy. If your puppy drops into a *down* position and is clearly more comfortable, there is nothing wrong with it. In the beginning, staying put is good enough!

The *Down* Command

Lying down is a great behavior to teach your puppy. If he's going to grow up to be a large dog, he won't be as intimidating to some people if he's lying down. It's also a convenient position in which to trim your puppy's nails. You may notice that some dogs will sit very quickly but will respond to the *down* command more slowly. Have patience and your pup will eventually learn to lie down when you ask.

With a puppy, it will be easier to teach the *down* if you are kneeling next to your dog. Have your dog sit and hold a treat in front of his nose. When his full attention is on the treat, start to lower the treat slowly to the ground, saying "Down." The dog should follow the treat with his head. Bring the treat out slowly in front of the pup. If you are really lucky, your puppy's legs will slide forward and he will lie down. Give him the treat and lots of praise for being such a good dog.

Some dogs learn particular skills in stages. If your dog lowers his body even a little bit while teaching the *down*, or moves his front feet forward without actually lying all the way down, you should still give him a "yes" indicator of correct behavior and reward him. With practice, he may eventually drop his body into a complete *down* in an effort to achieve comfort.

WALK NICELY ON LEASH

Dog walking is one of the most common and enjoyable activities for dog owners. It is a great way to get some exercise and fresh air and to socialize with neighbors. At the same time, nothing is more annoying than a dog who constantly pulls on the leash. Returning home with a sore arm and stiff shoulder is enough to take most of the fun out of a pleasurable stroll. Even though your puppy may not be a heavyweight right now, even small breed adults can still give a pretty strong, steady tug on a leash, making dog walking an uncomfortable experience.

Dogs have a faster pace than humans. When allowed to explore off leash, they will bound ahead as if in a great hurry to get somewhere. As a result, when they pull on a leash, they are simply attempting to move at a speed more natural to them. You can provide an effective consequence for this behavior by not allowing your puppy to pursue the direction he wants to go until he realizes he will not get there any faster by pulling. Giving your puppy appropriate rewards for keeping pace with you is also in order.

Teaching Walk Nicely on Leash

To encourage your puppy to stay close to you, hold a treat by your side as you walk and reward your pup frequently when he walks on a loose leash at your side. Each time your puppy pulls on the leash, abruptly turn around and start walking in the opposite direction. This interrupts the behavior and gets his attention. It also makes it clear to the puppy that he will not be getting anywhere by pulling.

It's imporant to teach your puppy to walk nicely on leash.

End on a High Note!

After a while, you should be able to move from one command to the next with no problem. If you run into a problem, it is probably because the puppy does not understand the command thoroughly, the training sessions are too long, or he is bored. Sometimes, the dog may just be having a bad day. If he just doesn't seem to be into the training session, do a simple exercise your dog knows well and call it a day. Be sure to use praise and play so that you end on a note of accomplishment.

Reward your puppy when he again approaches your side.

If you have a higher goal than simply teaching your dog to walk on a loose leash, use this same method to teach your dog to heel. This is a more precise obedience skill in which the dog handler holds the leash in her right hand while the dog walks close to the handler's left side. Encourage your dog to stay close to your left side by holding a treat in your left hand, and reward your dog frequently for maintaining his position there. If your dog gets out of position, turn around and walk in the opposite direction while commanding him to heel. When he comes back up to your side, reward him.

14

PROBLEM SOLVING

Dogs will be dogs. Behaviors that we may consider to be "problems" are often just puppies doing what puppies do. Things like barking, digging, and jumping up are natural puppy instincts. You must teach your dog what behavior you want in your home—he will not know automatically.

Basic obedience training is the first step toward controlling problem behaviors. All training should reinforce the rules you have set forth, as well as the understanding that by obeying you, your puppy will reap all sorts of benefits and rewards. Once your puppy knows these things, it should be fairly easy to control his behavior.

Remember that puppies have a seemingly unlimited amount of energy and will get into mischief if this energy is not properly directed. Puppies who are bored or restless will look for things to do, such as digging up your flower beds or running out the door when it's opened. If you provide your puppy with plenty of play and exercise, he will be too tired to get into trouble.

There are some common puppy behaviors that may cause problems in your house. The good news is that with the proper training and motivation, they can be dealt with easily.

BEFORE YOU START: GET A HEALTH CHECK

If your dog displays behavior problems, it may not be because of lack of training. Some experts feel that 20 percent of all behavior problems are health-related. Housetraining accidents could be caused

Twenty percent of problem behaviors may be health-related.

by bladder infections or gastrointestinal upset, and medical problems like thyroid imbalance can cause hyperactivity. Poor nutrition can also be a factor. Chewing on garden plants or wood could indicate that your puppy is not getting enough nutrients, and food allergies are often the cause of behavior problems. Before you start training your dog, make sure he has been to the veterinarian and has received a clean bill of health. Once health problems have been ruled out, you can start correcting any unwanted behavior.

Misplaced Aggression

Lacy was a Sheltie who seemed afraid of everything—I mean everything! She would attack the phone every time it rang and the kitchen cabinet every time the microwave finished heating a meal. Her family thought this was hilarious behavior and would laugh and laugh—even applaud—every time she did it. To Lacy, it was clear that her family was living in terror of these irritating noises until she came along. The fact that it made her family happy when she protected them just reinforced the behavior. Then she really couldn't understand why they were so mad at her when she destroyed the telephone and ate away most of the cabinet that held the microwave. Wasn't she just getting closer to solving everyone's problems? Lacy's behavior is an example of what happens when you reinforce your puppy's aggression toward new objects or noises. If her family had ignored the behavior and redirected her to something else, like a toy or a bone, they might not be remodeling their kitchen right now.

AGGRESSION

Aggression is the most serious behavioral problem owners will encounter. Protective breeds can be more aggressive than others, but with the proper upbringing and training, they can make very dependable companions. Many factors contribute to aggression, including genetics and environment. An improper environment, which may include poor living conditions, lack of socialization, excessive punishment, or being attacked or frightened, can all influence a dog's behavior. Some owners may even unwittingly reinforce aggressive behavior. Isolation, lack of human contact, or exposure to frequent teasing by children or adults also can ruin a good dog.

In addition, lack of direction, fear, or confusion can lead to aggression in those dogs who are so inclined. Any obedience exercises, such as the *sit* and the *down*, can redirect the puppy's attention and help him overcome any fear or confusion. When your puppy shows signs of aggression, you should speak calmly (no screaming or hysterics) and firmly give a command he understands, such as the *sit*. This will help redirect your puppy. Some puppies show too much aggression for their owners to handle. If caution is exercised and professional help is gained early on, most cases can be controlled.

If you have done everything according to the book regarding training and socialization and are still dealing with a behavior problem, don't procrastinate. The problem needs to receive professional attention before it gets out of hand.

BARKING

Some owners think that they want their

dog to bark—that it makes the puppy a good watchdog. However, this is a habit that should not be encouraged. Most dogs will bark anyway when a stranger comes to the door or into their territory. What you don't want is a dog who barks at every car that drives by or every leaf that falls into the yard. This is not only annoying to you but to the entire neighborhood as well.

Managing the Problem

Barking can be a problem in some breeds or a bad habit that is acquired. It takes the owner's dedication to stop a dog's barking. First, you should figure out the cause. Is the dog seeking attention or does he need to go out? Is it feeding time, is the dog alone, or is it a protective bark? If the barking seems to be caused by something simple, like barking to go outside or because the dog is hungry, it should be easy to control this behavior.

Barking can be a problem in some breeds or a bad habit that is acquired.

Overzealous barking can be an inherited tendency, but a lot of puppy barking is due to boredom. If your puppy barks for attention or when left alone, you can take steps to stop it. If you notice that your puppy barks for attention, you must not reinforce the bad behavior. Never give attention when he is barking. Wait until the dog is quiet, and then use petting and praise. If the barking starts again, walk away and ignore the pup. He should get the picture in no time. If you notice that your dog barks when left alone, there are a few things you can try. Before you leave, see that the pup has been walked, fed, and given water. Be sure to allow plenty of time for exercise before you leave—a sleeping puppy will not be a barking puppy. Make sure you curb your dog's boredom by providing him with lots of toys while you're gone. Leave a radio tuned to an easy-listening station for company. Pull the shades or close the curtains. Eventually, the dog will get used to time alone, especially if he's having fun all alone.

BITING/NIPPING

All puppies bite and try to chew on your fingers, toes, arms, etc. This is the time to teach them to be gentle and not to bite hard.

Managing the Problem

If your fingers end up your puppy's mouth and he bites too hard, say "Easy!" Let the pup know he's hurting you by squealing and acting like you have been seriously hurt. Do not continue to play until he has calmed down.

Biting in the more mature dog is something that should be prevented at

All puppies try to chew on fingers; you'll need to teach your puppy to be gentle.

all costs. If it occurs, you should seek professional help at once, either through your veterinarian, dog trainer, and/or behaviorist. A dog bite is serious and should be given immediate attention. Wash the bite with soap and water and contact your doctor. It is important to know the status of the offender's rabies vaccination.

BORN TO RUN

If dogs are never let off leash except when supervised in a fenced-in yard, they can't do much running away. However,

there is always the dog who seems to have been an escape artist in another life and will get out no matter how diligent you are.

Managing the Problem

Perhaps your puppy escapes while you are both playing in the yard and refuses to come when called. If your puppy is not in immediate danger, the best thing is to use a little reverse psychology. Do not chase your dog; he will just think that you are playing a game and will run farther. Use what you know, namely that your dog loves to be with you. Puppies never want to miss out on the fun. Try calling his name in a happy, excited tone of voice and then running in the opposite direction. Most likely, your curious puppy will want in on the game and start to

Keeping your puppy leashed or in a safely enclosed yard will help prevent escapes.

follow you. You can then turn around and call him to you. Always kneel down when trying to catch the runaway because dogs can be intimidated by people standing over them. It is always helpful to have a treat or a favorite toy to help entice the pup to your side.

Remember that when you finally do catch your naughty dog, you must not use discipline. After all, there could be a repeat performance, and it would be nice if next time your dog would respond to your *come* command.

Until the dog responds reliably to the *come* command every time, attach a long line to him. The puppy will not be able to judge how long the line is, and you can grab the line without getting too close

or step on it to stop the dog. Then just reel in your "fish" with a big smile and lots of praise. As the dog matures and masters basic obedience, he will realize it is a pleasure to be at your side and will eagerly come every time you call.

CHEWING

Puppies and adolescent dogs are especially prone to chewing. Your puppy's deciduous (baby) teeth begin to come in when he is about four weeks old. When he's four to five months old, his deciduous teeth loosen, fall out, and are replaced by permanent (adult) teeth. During this process, his gums become swollen and sore, and he'll chew whatever he can grab to relieve his discomfort.

Some dogs continue to enjoy chewing throughout their lives; others rarely chew as adults.

Managing the Problem

As with other problem behaviors, prevention is the ideal treatment. Begin by putting anything you don't want him to grab out of his reach. Don't underestimate a determined puppy! Locked away out of sight is much safer than simply placed up high—some breeds have been known to scale amazing heights to snatch things from shelves and other elevated areas.

After you have done this, teach your dog that he may chew some things but not everything. If he picks up something he

Set your puppy up for success by removing anything you don't want him to chew on.

shouldn't, take it from him gently and give him one of his toys. Don't yell or punish him. That won't teach him what's right, and it may lead to other unwanted behaviors. Be smart, too—don't give him old shoes or socks to play with and then pretend you're surprised when he chews your good ones! Be consistent and think ahead, and your puppy will soon learn what he's allowed to do.

If your puppy is prone to chewing and ripping things, then he should never be left unsupervised where he can get to things he shouldn't have. This is a simple and sensible solution, and it's much kinder than letting your dog chew something that injures him. Confine your puppy to his crate with a nice chew toy to play with when you can't watch him.

COPROPHAGIA (EATING FECES)

Puppies usually love the taste of feces. It's unappetizing but true. They'll eat their own poop, and if you have other dogs, they'll eat their feces, too. Horse manure can be especially tempting. And if you have a cat, well, cat poop is a delicacy to your puppy! The habit of eating stools is called coprophagia.

Not every puppy develops this habit. But if your puppy is eating poop, it's a bigger problem than just bad breath and nasty puppy kisses. He could ingest intestinal parasites and get sick. Puppies who eat large amounts of horse manure can develop severe diarrhea and vomiting.

Usually, puppies who develop coprophagia are not suffering from any nutritional deficiencies. In other words, there's nothing missing in their diets that causes them to crave poop. They can develop the habit out of boredom, from being raised in close confinement that isn't properly cleaned, or because of something as simple as they tried it one day and liked the taste.

Managing the Problem

There are theories about adding things to your puppy's diet to make the taste of his poop less appealing. You can purchase these products from pet stores or your veterinarian. You also may have heard about adding things to his food, from meat tenderizer to pineapple to pumpkin. Some people experience success with these items; others have no success at all.

A surefire way to solve the problem is through good management. As soon as your puppy eliminates, pick it up and deposit it in a waste receptacle out of his reach. If you have other dogs, pick up after them right away, too. Put your litter box in a place where your cat can access it but your puppy can't. If you are around horses, keep your puppy on leash and make sure that he does not get near any horse manure. If he never has access to poop, he can't eat it and thus can't get sick from it. It may be a bit more work to clean up after your puppy promptly, but it's healthier for everyone in your family.

Some dogs crave stool for a few rare medical reasons. If you have concerns, always check with your veterinarian. Never rub your puppy's nose in his stool or scream at him for eating poop. Yes, it's a disgusting habit—to you, not to your puppy. He thinks it's delicious! Just manage the issue and train him to leave his stools alone.

DIGGING

Many dogs like to dig. If your puppy smells or hears evidence of little furry animals under the surface of the ground,

Many dogs like to dig.

he'll want to unearth them. If he has a bone or other treasure, he might decide to bury it. If you leave your puppy alone in the yard, he might try his paw at landscaping to relieve his boredom and expend his energy.

Managing the Problem

A determined digger can quickly turn a lovely yard into a moonscape, and you almost certainly will want to keep that from happening where you live. You could supervise all of your dog's outdoor time, but that's not a practical solution for most people. Fortunately, you can discourage and redirect inappropriate digging. Some of these methods work with some dogs (not all), but if

Some breeds are more prone to digging than others.

you're at least as smart and determined as your puppy, you can have your dog and a normal yard as well.

Not all breeds are serious diggers, but if yours is, why not give him his own personal recreational digging spot? Pick a place with loose sand or sandy soil, which is cleaner than clay or loam and a lot more fun to send flying. Build your dog a sandbox if necessary, making sure the sand is deep enough that he can really dig in and that you have a barrier to control the flying sand or dirt. Bury a toy or treat, bring your pup to the spot, and let him sniff. Encourage him to dig and praise him when he does. Then, encourage him to find the buried treasure. Repeat the process over a few days. In the meantime, if you see your dog digging in a different part of the yard, say "Leave it" and take him to his permitted digging

spot. Don't leave him alone in the yard until you're confident that he won't dig in the wrong places.

If your puppy tends to dig in one particular illegal spot, try filling or covering his hole with rocks, a pot, or some other dig-proof barrier. You can also bury chicken wire under the top layer of soil in a garden—plants will still be able to grow, but your dog's digging will be curtailed. Fencing or wire buried horizontally or vertically also helps keep dogs from tunneling under fences.

JUMPING UP

A puppy who jumps up is a happy puppy. However, while it's cute when the dog is small, few guests appreciate dogs jumping on them, especially when your sweet little Great Dane pup continues this habit into adulthood. There will come a time, probably around four months of age, when your puppy will need to know when it is okay to jump and when good manners, such as sitting, are better.

Managing the Problem

How do you correct the problem? Teach the puppy the *sit* command as soon as he starts to jump up. The *sit* must be practiced every time your dog starts to jump up. Don't forget to give lots of praise for good behavior. Remember that the entire family must take part by reinforcing the sit. Each time you allow the dog to jump, you go back a step in training, because your puppy will not understand that it is okay to jump on some people but not others.

FEAR

One of the most common problems that puppies experience is fear reactions. Some dogs are more afraid than others, depending on their temperament, the socialization that they have received, and their early environment. Sometimes, dogs can be afraid of a strange object, which can be humorous to watch. They act silly when something is out of place in the house. This problem is called perceptive intelligence. Dogs realize the abnormal within their known environment. They may not react the same way in strange environments because they do not know what is normal.

A jumping puppy may seem cute now, but this behavior could be a problem when he's older and larger.

Attack Poodles?

One trainer told me about a problem she had with two Poodles, Sugar and Spice. They were as adorable and tiny as could be. Their owner figured that there wasn't any harm in letting them run everywhere and bark at everything. She even thought it was kind of cute when all 5 pounds (2 kg) of Sugar and Spice would protect the living room couch and maul whoever sat there—after all, what damage could they do? After six months of their constant barking and refusing to walk on a leash, the owner had two tiny, uncontrollable terrors and a living room she couldn't enter. She finally decided to seek professional help. The moral of the story is that no matter what their size, basic training is essential to help dogs develop into well-mannered adults who are pleasurable to live with.

A more serious fear is a fear of people. This can result in behavior that includes backing away or hiding, or it can result in an aggressive behavior that may lead to challenging a person or fear biting. This can really be a problem if there are young, rambunctious children in the house who may unintentionally frighten or overwhelm the puppy.

Managing the Problem

Hopefully, you have chosen a puppy who has a temperament that fits in with your household. The best type of household for a pup who displays fear or timidity is one with adults who will respect the puppy's feelings. If your puppy is timid of new situations or people, respect that the dog wants to be left alone and allow time for him to come forward. If you approach, the cornered dog may resort to snapping. Left alone, the dog may decide to come out voluntarily, which should be rewarded with a treat.

Dogs can be afraid of numerous things, including loud noises and thunderstorms. Invariably, the owner rewards the dog's fearfulness by comforting him. Instead, direct your dog's attention to something else and act perfectly normal. For example, if your puppy is barking at the new plant in the living room, simply go up to the plant, touch it, and say something in a happy tone of voice. Don't dwell on the fright. Act normally and show him that there is nothing to be afraid of.

SUBMISSIVE URINATION

Submissive urination is not a housetraining problem but rather a psychological problem. It can occur in all breeds and may be more prevalent in some. Usually it occurs in puppies and may be in response to physical praise or overexcitement. Many dogs outgrow this problem, and scolding will only make the problem worse. Try verbal praise instead of physical petting for a while, and make sure that your dog has had a chance to urinate outdoors before playing with you.

PART FOUR

HAVING FUN

WITH YOUR PUPPY

15

TRAVELING WITH (OR WITHOUT) YOUR PUPPY

One of the best things about getting a new puppy is that you have a companion who can accompany you on any adventure. You might bring your puppy on a fun family vacation, or you may travel with him to participate in a canine activity. Other times you may have to leave your pup at home. With good planning, you and your pup will be ready for just about anything!

CAR TRAVEL

The first step to getting out there and trying new experiences is making sure that your pup can travel with you. Your puppy must become used to everyday travel in order to go to the veterinarian, the groomer, and even better, the dog park. Also, at some point you will have to decide whether or not the puppy will accompany the family on vacation. Puppyhood is the time to start acclimating your dog to new surroundings. The earlier you start, the better.

A puppy who has good experiences in the car from the start should have no problems. In fact, most dogs love to take a ride and will eagerly jump into the back seat. All I have to say to my dog, Chester, is, "Wanna go…?" and he's sitting by the car door. In fact, with most dogs, you can't even open the car door when they're around because they'll jump right in and refuse to get out!

The best way to ensure that your dog has the same reaction is to make all car rides pleasant. This doesn't mean that you should never take your puppy to the vet for shots, but make sure that's not the only place you both go in the car, either. When you do go to the vet, the groomer,

or anywhere else that may be unpleasant, make sure you also stop at the beach or park on the way home as a reward.

The safest place for your puppy when he's in the car is in a crate. They also make harnesses, dog seat belts, and barriers for the back of cars to keep your puppy safe and secure while traveling. A dog who roams all over the car can even interfere with your driving and injure you both. You can pay better attention to the road when you know that your dog is secure and safe in one spot.

Unfortunately, some dogs aren't very good travelers. Perhaps they associate the car with leaving their mother

Car harnesses can keep your puppy safe during travel.

or with trips to the veterinarian. Others may be nervous riders and get carsick. These dogs need special conditioning in order to make them good travelers. The best thing to do for these pups is to slowly recondition them to enjoy the time they spend in the car.

Car Travel Tips

The following procedures should help your puppy get used to road travel:

- Make sure you allow ample time outside before you and your pup get in the car. This will help prevent accidents.
- Do not feed your pup for a few hours before you start traveling. Also, allow for plenty of air circulation throughout the car to avoid overheating or stuffiness.
- Place your puppy in the car for a few moments while it is parked in the driveway. Let him out, and then offer a treat. Do this every day for about a week or until your puppy looks forward to sitting in the car. (Of course, getting the treat has a lot to do with it!)
- Once your puppy is content sitting in the car, drive to the end of the driveway or down the block and back. When you let him out, offer a treat. Do this for about a week or until your puppy willingly gets in the car for short rides.
- Once your puppy seems totally comfortable with very short rides, gradually make them longer. Always end by giving a treat or by driving a short distance to a fun destination.
- It may be slow going at first, but if you are patient and make the trips fun and rewarding, your puppy will be traveling like a pro in no time.

No Parking
Never, ever leave your dog unattended in a car. Temperatures can climb to life-threatening levels very quickly, even if the windows are partially rolled down and the dog has access to drinking water. Your dog can suffer from heatstroke in a very short time, so if you can't bring your dog with you when you leave the car, leave him at home.

AIR TRAVEL

Let's face it, dogs are happiest with all four feet on the ground. Airline travel can be stressful for your puppy. On some airlines, puppies and small dogs are allowed to travel with you in the cabin if they can fit under the seat and are properly contained. However, most dogs will have to fly in the cargo hold, where they can be subjected to temperature changes, flight delays, and other difficulties. Most experts recommend that puppies not fly, but if it cannot be avoided, there are ways to make the flight easier.

First, you need to get an airline-approved crate. Federal guidelines on crate size and construction must be adhered to. Crates need to be sturdy, properly ventilated, contain water and food dishes, and most importantly, be large enough for the animal to freely stand, turn around, and lie down. To prevent injury, no part of the animal's body should protrude through any openings of the crate. For this reason, crates made exclusively of wire are not advisable. A "Live Animal" label with letters at least 1 inch (2 cm) high must be placed on the crate, along with arrows indicating which end is up. If your dog is not crate trained, slowly introduce the crate long before the flight.

Second, take your dog to the vet at least 30 days before you travel. Health certificates are required for all pets transported by air and are usually valid for 30 days for domestic flights and 10 days for international flights.

It is also important to advise the airline that you are traveling with an animal when you make your reservations. Be sure to reconfirm with the airline 24 to 48 hours

Some puppies and small dogs can fly in the cabin with you provided you have the appropriate carrier.

before departure that you will be bringing your pet. Advance arrangements are not a guarantee that your animal will travel on a specific flight, so be vigilant about confirming that your pet will travel with you on the same flight all the way.

Lots of pets travel safely every year by air. If you follow the proper guidelines, air travel should be less stressful for all involved.

Preparing for Flight

Listed below are some helpful travel tips from the Animal and Plant Health Inspection Service (APHIS), an agency of the US Department of Agriculture. APHIS enforces regulations ensuring that animals traveling by air are treated humanely by airlines.

- If you are sending your pet through the cargo system, you will need to go to the cargo terminal, which is usually located in a separate part of the airport. Be sure to check with your airline for the

acceptance cutoff time for your flight. By regulation, an animal may be present for transport no more than four hours before flight time.

- Use direct flights whenever possible to avoid accidental transfers or delays.
- Remember that some dogs are more likely to experience breathing problems during air travel, such as short-nosed breeds like Bulldogs.
- Instructions for feeding and watering an animal over a 24-hour period must be attached to the kennel. The 24-hour schedule will assist the airline in providing care in case your dog is diverted from the original destination.
- Carry a leash with you so that you can walk your pet before check-in and after arrival. Do not place the leash inside the kennel or attach it to the outside of the kennel—keep it with you.
- Outfit your pet with a sturdy collar and two identification tags. The tags should have both your permanent address and telephone number and an address and telephone number where you can be reached while traveling.
- Attach a label on the pet carrier with your permanent and travel addresses and telephone numbers.
- Make sure your pet's nails have been recently clipped to prevent snagging on the carrier door or other openings.
- Carry a current photograph of your pet. If he is accidentally lost, this will make the search easier.
- Most of all, don't be afraid to speak up. Let the crew know that your pet is traveling with you and that his safety is crucial.

- If you need to file a complaint regarding the care of your pet during transport, contact USDA-APHIS-Animal Care.

ON YOUR WAY

Once your puppy is used to traveling, life is an open road! There are many destinations in the US and in Canada that welcome canine travelers. If you decide to take an extended road trip with your puppy, the following tips will make your vacation a little easier on everyone.

Before you hit the road, your puppy should know basic obedience commands and be leash trained. Any dog should be leashed whenever out of the car. This is because you'll most likely be stopping in rest areas that have lots of traffic, and you will encounter new people and places that could possibly scare the dog. Remember to bring enough food to last the entire trip. If you run out, you might not be able to find the brand your puppy normally eats, and a quick switch in food can cause an upset stomach or diarrhea, making the trip miserable for all of you.

Pack His Bags!

Pack the car not only for the humans on the trip but also for your dog. For many dog owners, the biggest challenge when it comes to packing is knowing when to say when. Pack too little and you might overlook something important, but bring too much and you might not have room for your puppy. So how do you determine which items warrant a spot on the list? When packing for my own dogs, I ask myself the following: Do they use this item every day, or would they need it in an emergency? If the answer to either of these questions is yes, it goes along with us.

What your puppy needs while on the road will depend on your individual circumstances, but here is a partial list of what to pack for most puppies:
- An up-to-date photograph in case your dog ever becomes lost
- Brush and comb
- Crate and blanket or padded insert
- Dog license, identification tag (firmly attached to your puppy's collar), and proof of current vaccinations
- First-aid kit and any necessary medications (including preventive treatments)
- Food (for when you reach your destination) and a full water container (for the ride)
- Food and water bowls
- Leash and collar
- Name and number of veterinary hospitals and emergency clinics in the area where you will be staying
- Plastic bags and baby wipes
- Towel
- Toys

ACCOMMODATIONS

Just a decade ago, the idea of finding a hotel that allowed pets was a virtual impossibility. If you were lucky enough to know of such a place, it was likely less than a four-star establishment, to say the least. Fortunately, the hospitality industry has made great strides in recent years by going that extra mile to accommodate their guests—people just like you and me who, as it happens, are also dog lovers. Petswelcome.com, a website that lists a variety of dog-friendly lodging, is an excellent resource for dog owners planning to travel with their pets. In addition to providing travelers with a directory of pet-friendly hotels and motels across the country, the site also offers information on campgrounds, beaches, and even long-term apartments that allow animals.

Don't forget to pack your puppy's essentials.

LEAVING YOUR PUPPY BEHIND

You might find it best to leave your pup at home when you travel for days at a time. There are a few options you can choose to make sure your puppy is comfortable and well taken care of when you're not there.

Pet Sitters

Pet care providers can come to your house once or twice a day to feed, walk, and play with your pet while you're away. The best part about this type of service is that animals get to stay at home where they feel most comfortable and can keep their daily routine.

When hiring a pet sitter, interview several candidates before making a decision. Remember that this person will have the responsibility for both your pet and home, so making the right selection is important. You should find out if the pet sitter is bonded, has commercial liability insurance, and will provide references. Ask for documented proof of these and check references. Services offered and fees charged can vary widely depending on what state you live in or even what town.

Once you've hired a sitter, let her know your puppy's daily eating, sleeping, and exercising schedule. Health problems should also be disclosed, as well as any medication your pet needs.

Pet Sitter Tips

To make sure everything runs smoothly while you're away, advanced planning is recommended. The following tips should help your pet sitter better care for your puppy:

- Make an extra copy of your house key

Hiring a pet sitter can be a great option when you can't bring your puppy with you.

for the sitter, and make sure it works. As a backup, give another copy to a neighbor. Let your sitter know the name and phone number of this neighbor.

- Buy extra food and supplies just in case you stay away longer than anticipated.
- Leave a list of phone numbers, such as your veterinarian and the place where you are staying while away.
- All food, leashes, and medicines should be left in one area so they are easy to locate.
- If the sitter will be visiting in the evenings, provide a timer light so that she won't have to walk into a dark house. It will probably make your pet more comfortable as well.

- If you will be returning earlier or later than expected, call to inform your sitter.
- Unplug any appliances that won't be used to prevent damage during electrical storms or injury to pets.

Boarding Kennels

Placing your pet in a boarding kennel is another option if you must travel for an extended period of time. Family, friends, coworkers, and your veterinarian are all good places to start your search for a well-run boarding kennel. Find out what they liked and disliked about the establishment, as well as how long they've used the facility. Consider using the resources available to find licensed boarding kennels throughout the US.

Once you have some leads, make an unannounced visit to check out the facility. The first place you'll want to see is where the animals are kept. If you're not allowed to view this area, for whatever reason, find another place. A reputable operator should never have a problem with showing the facility to a potential client; it could indicate a disorganized, unkempt place.

Most importantly, ask if the facility accepts puppies. Also ask if it accepts puppies who are on medication or who require special handling, if necessary. If they do, find out if there is an extra fee for these special cases.

As you tour the kennel, you'll want to take note of a few things. The fencing used for runs should be in good shape and smooth, with no sharp edges. There should be a solid barrier between runs high enough to prevent physical contact

Professional Pet Sitters

Professional pet sitters are people who have trained to watch animals and are bonded and accredited with a pet-sitting organization, like Pet Sitters International. Professional pet sitters are acquainted with pet health and training, and they have likely taken courses about all aspects of pet care, including disaster preparation and planning. Many have insurance as well.

and cross urination. Also, if you have an escape artist puppy, make sure the runs have covers and that the bottoms of the fences are secure. The sleeping area of a run should be roomy enough for your pet to stand up comfortably, turn around in, and easily stretch out.

Overall, the facility should be clean, well lit, and odorless. Kennels should be disinfected daily with a cleaning solution, like diluted bleach, then rinsed thoroughly and allowed to dry before an animal is let back into the run to prevent chemical burns. The temperature should be set to a comfortable level. There should also be a good ventilation system, which allows fresh air to circulate into the kennel area.

While touring the facility, find out how often the dogs are checked during the day and if there is a play area for exercise. Also, check to see if your dog will have an individual run or if he will be sharing it. A good kennel should honor the request for a dog to be boarded alone.

Ask what brand of food is used. Some facilities only stock one type, while others have several popular varieties in order to match their clients' regular fare. If they don't have your dog's brand, find out if you can bring in a supply. Sticking with your dog's regular diet is important because a sudden change can cause an upset stomach and/or diarrhea.

Find out how they handle health situations and veterinary procedures. What is their policy if the kennel staff notices any health problems, such as vomiting, dehydration, or bloody stool or urine? Will they take the dog to your regular veterinarian or use their own?

Check which methods of payment they accept and what their hours of operation are. Some facilities might be closed on weekends and certain holidays, which means if you return home on those days, you won't be able to pick up your pet until the next day.

Usually boarders are required to be vaccinated for rabies, distemper, parvovirus, hepatitis, leptospirosis, parainfluenza, and bordetella or kennel cough. Ask if there are any other types of vaccinations required and what proof you'll need to show that your dog has had the proper immunizations.

After your visit and before making a decision on what facility to use, take into consideration whether the staff was friendly and if the establishment was well run and organized. The more you know about the facility, the easier you will feel about your puppy's welfare while you are away.

If you have to board your puppy, see if you can provide his regular food.

16

ORGANIZED SPORTS AND EVENTS

O nce your puppy has completed basic obedience training, there are many different activities that you can participate in together. Almost all dogs have special skills for which they were originally bred. The trick is to find the perfect match: Find the sport that your dog has a natural talent for and enjoys doing and that you enjoy doing together. Once you find that perfect combination, there is no end to how far you and your puppy can go.

BEFORE YOU GET STARTED

It is important to remember that very young puppies are still growing; their bones are soft, and they may not be fully developed until they are a year old or more. Hold off on any serious workouts until your puppy has fully matured physically, as he may suffer permanent damage.

Before you decide to participate in any activity, your puppy should have a thorough veterinary checkup. For any athletic sport, you must make sure that your puppy's body is sound and healthy enough to participate. Although you can familiarize your puppy with some of the elements of a particular activity (like retrieving, catching, basic obedience) from a very young age, you should not participate in many sports until he is grown and his bones are mature. For example, the high leaps that dogs achieve to catch a flying disc require strong spines, hips, knees, and legs for safe landings.

AGILITY

One of the fastest growing, most popular, and fun events is agility. It was developed and introduced in 1978 in England by John Varley and Peter Meanwell as an entertaining diversion between judgings at dog shows, but it was officially recognized as a sport by the American Kennel Club (AKC) in the early 1980s. Agility is an exciting sport in which you guide your dog off-leash using verbal commands and hand signals over a series of obstacles on a timed course.

Agility trial titles are Novice Agility Dog (NAD), Open Agility Dog (OAD), Agility Dog Excellent (ADX), and Master Agility Excellent (MAX). In order to acquire an agility title, your dog must earn three qualifying scores in each class

You can teach your puppy some of the agility obstacles but need to wait until his bones are mature to work on jumps.

under two different judges. The MAX title is awarded after the dog earns ten qualifying scores in the Agility Excellent Class.

This puppy is learning how to pose for the show ring.

The only problem with training your puppy to compete in agility is finding the equipment and space to train. Many agility clubs can provide information on getting started toward an agility title. Even if you don't compete, just training for agility can be lots of fun for both you and your dog.

Agility is regulated by dog registries. The AKC offers agility competition for purebred dogs. The United Kennel Club (UKC), the North American Dog Agility Council (NADAC), the United States Dog Agility Association (USDAA), and the Australian Shepherd Club of America (ASCA) also offer agility competition, and all of them offer agility to mixed-breed dogs.

To participate safely in agility, your puppy should get a clearance from his veterinarian. This is a very athletic sport, so you want to make sure that your puppy's body is sound enough to participate. He can begin to learn some agility obstacles at a young age, but he should wait until his bones are mature before you teach him any of the jumps.

CONFORMATION

Everyone thinks that they have a good-looking puppy. If your dog is an AKC-registered purebred and is six months of age or older, you may want to jump into the world of dog showing. You may have even purchased your puppy from a breeder with the intent of getting into conformation. In conformation, the main consideration is overall appearance and structure and how closely the dog conforms to the official standard of perfection for the breed.

If you would like to get involved in showing, the first thing you should do is go to dog shows in your area without your dog. Spend the day watching not only your breed's judging but others as well. Judges examine the dogs and place them according to how close each one compares with the ideal dog as described in the breed's official standard. These judges are experts in the breeds they are judging. They examine each dog with their hands to see if the teeth, muscles, bones, and coat texture match the standard. Each dog is examined in profile for general balance and watched while moving to see how all these features fit together.

How Dog Shows Work

There are three types of conformation shows: Specialty, Group, and All-breed. Specialty shows are limited to a specific breed. Group shows are limited to dogs from one of the seven groups (for example, an all-terrier show). All-breed shows are open to the 164 breeds recognized by the AKC. Most dogs at conformation shows are competing for points toward a championship. It takes 15 points, including two major wins (3, 4, or 5 points) under at least three different judges to become an AKC Champion of Record, which is indicated by a "Ch." before the dog's name.

At one show, a non-champion dog can earn from one to five points, depending on the number actually defeated. There are six different regular classes in which dogs may be entered, and these are offered to male and female dogs separately in each breed. Once a champion, the dog can compete for Best of Breed without having to win in any other class.

After these classes are judged, the first-place winner in each class competes for the championship points. This is done separately for male and female dogs. Only the best male, Winners Dog, and the best female, Winners Bitch, receive championship points. A Reserve Winner award is given in each sex to the runner-up. The Winners Dog and the Winners Bitch then compete with the champions for Best of Breed. At the end of the Best of Breed competition, three awards are usually given. Best of Breed is given to the dog judged best in each breed. Best of Winners is awarded to either the Winners Dog or the Winners Bitch, and Best of Opposite Sex is given to the best of the opposite sex to the Best of Breed winner.

Only the Best of Breed winners advance to compete in the Group competition. Each breed falls into one of seven Group classifications. Four placements are awarded in each Group, but only the first place winner advances to the Best in Show competition.

Dog showing can be a very rewarding experience. But be careful—once bitten by the show bug, many people get addicted!

Junior Showmanship

If your children are interested in training and competing, you may want to get involved in Junior Showmanship, which evolved as part of the concept that dog shows should be a family sport as well as entertainment. It was started in the 1930s and has continually grown in participation. It is now an integral part of almost every dog show held in the US and other countries. It is a great way to teach children how to handle, care for, and respect their pets and also gives them a good start in the sport of dog showing. Participating in Junior Showmanship deepens the unique relationship between children and their dogs.

The AKC rules state that the dog entered in a Junior Showmanship class must be owned by the junior, a member of the immediate family, or someone from the same household. Every dog entered must be eligible to compete in either conformation or obedience, which means the dog must be registered with the AKC. This does not mean that the dog must be of top quality. The rules state that entries in this activity are not judged on the quality of the dog but on the ability of the junior handler only.

The classes are Novice Junior and Novice Senior, and Open Junior and Open Senior. The Novice Junior class is for boys and girls who are at least 10 but under 14 years of age on the day of the show and who have not won three first-place awards in a Novice class at a licensed or member show. The Novice Senior class is for boys and girls who are at least 14 but under 18 years of age and who have not won three first-place awards in a Novice class. The Open Junior class is for boys and girls who are at least 10 but under 14 years of age on the day of the show and who have won three first-place awards in a Novice class.

Some activities may have to wait until your puppy has had all his shots, like those activities that require that you go out in public places. Some may have to wait until his body is more mature and stronger, such as some of the active sporting activities.

The Open Senior class is for boys and girls who are at least 14 but under 18 years of age on the day of the show and have won three first-place awards in a Novice class.

DANCING WITH DOGS

Canine musical freestyle is a relatively new competitive sport that combines obedience and dance to display teamwork and rapport between dog and handler. Routines are set to music, and the handler interprets the music with body, arm, and leg motions while the dog performs various movements. The handlers and many of the dogs wear costumes. The emphasis in competition is on teamwork between the handler and the dog, both of whom are judged.

The World Canine Freestyle Organization (WCFO) offers titles in three divisions. Singles Division (one dog and one handler) competitors can earn the titles W-FD (Freestyle Dog), W-FDX (Freestyle Dog Excellent), W-FDM (Freestyle Dog Master), and W-Ch.FD (Champion Freestyle Dog). Pairs Division (two dogs and two handlers) participants can earn the W-PFD, W-PFDX, W-PFDM, and W-PchFD, with "P" indicating "pairs." Team competitors (multiple dogs, each with a handler) can earn the titles W-TD, W-FDX, W-TFDM, and W-TCh.FD.

Musical Canine Sports International (MCSI) offers titles in Individual (one handler, one dog), Brace (two handlers, two dogs), and Team (three or more handlers, each with a dog) classes with On-leash and Off-leash divisions at three levels. Dogs can earn the titles of MFD (Musical Freestyle Dog), MFX (Musical Freestyle Excellent), and MFM (Musical Freestyle Master) based on qualifying scores in each of the different classes. You may begin in any class and division but must qualify from the Off-leash Division to enter Masters.

DRAFT WORK AND CARTING

In many parts of the world, beasts of burden like horses and oxen were not easy to come by. Therefore, breeds like the Newfoundland, Bouvier des Flandres, Alaskan Malamute, and Bernese Mountain Dog have been used for thousands of years as cart pullers, sled dogs, and draft dogs. These breeds can still show their inherent talents and strength by participating in sled and carting competitions and draft tests. If your breed is one that historically has had this ability and is physically fit, you can contact the breed club in your area to find out more about how to begin training for these events. Once trained, your dog can use these skills not only in organized events but also in helping you with hauling and yard work.

EARTHDOG TRIALS

Does your terrier or Dachshund pup love to dig holes and chase rabbits in your backyard? If so, you may have a natural candidate for earthdog trials. Earthdog trials are for the "go-to-ground" breeds (the smaller terriers and Dachshunds) that were originally bred to go into dens and tunnels after prey, which consisted of all types of small vermin, from rats to badgers. There are four class levels at a licensed trial: Introduction to Quarry (for beginning handlers and dogs), Junior Earthdog, Senior Earthdog, and Master Earthdog. The object of the test is to give your dog an opportunity to display the ability to follow game and to "work" the quarry. The "work" is showing interest in the game by barking, digging, and scratching. The quarry can either be two adult rats, who must be caged to be protected from the dogs, or artificial quarry that is located behind a barrier, properly scented, and capable of movement. The dogs eligible to participate in earthdog trials are Dachshunds, as well as these terriers: Australian, Bedlington, Border, Cairn, Dandie Dinmont, Fox (Smooth and Wire), Lakeland, Norfolk, Norwich, Parson Russell, Scottish, Sealyham, Silky, Skye, Welsh, and West Highland White.

If your puppy has draft work in his genes, like this Bernese Mountain Dog, carting may be a great sport to try.

FIELD EVENTS

The American Kennel Club runs field trials and hunt tests that are open to pointing breeds, retrievers, spaniels, Basset Hounds, Beagles, and Dachshunds over the age of six months and registered with the AKC. Individual clubs sponsor these events under AKC sanction or license. If you own any of the eligible breeds, it is quite a thrill to see your puppy develop and demonstrate those natural instincts.

In hunt tests, the dog's ability to perform is judged against a standard of perfection established by AKC regulations. Dogs who receive qualifying scores at a number of tests achieve titles of JH (Junior Hunter), SH (Senior Hunter), and MH (Master Hunter), each successively requiring more skill.

Beagling events involve trailing game.

In field trials, dogs compete against each other for placements and points toward field championships. Successful dogs earn an FC (Field Champion) title in front of their names. The field events are divided by subgroups of dogs and are sometimes limited to specific breeds. Each type of event varies according to a breed's function. These events include:

- **Beagling:** Currently, there are three types of trials: Brace, the oldest, is run in braces of two or three dogs who are judged primarily on their accuracy trailing a rabbit; Small Pack Option (SPO), which divides the dogs into packs of seven to pursue rabbits; and Large Pack, which turn all the dogs in the class loose to find and track hares.
- **Basset Hounds and Dachshunds:** These trials are run in a similar fashion as the Beagle Brace trials but are held separately.

- **Pointing Breeds:** The AKC offers pointing breed field trials and hunt tests. The dogs are run in braces around a course on which birds are released. Dogs must demonstrate their ability to find birds, point, and retrieve the downed birds. The eligible pointing breeds are the Brittany, English Setter, German Shorthaired Pointer, Gordon Setter, Irish Setter, Pointer, Vizsla, Weimaraner, and Wirehaired Pointing Griffon.

- **Retrievers:** Retrievers are tested on their ability to remember or "mark" the location of downed birds and to return the birds to their handlers. Both the hunt tests and the field trials have different levels of difficulty, requiring dogs to mark multiple birds and find unmarked birds, called blind retrieves. Breeds that are eligible for these trials are the Chesapeake, Curly-Coated, Flat-Coated, Golden, and Labrador Retrievers, and the Irish Water Spaniel.

- **Spaniels:** Spaniels are judged on their natural and learned ability to hunt, flush, and retrieve game on both land and water. Breeds that are eligible for hunt tests are the Clumber, Cocker, English Cocker, English Springer, Sussex, and Welsh Springer Spaniels. Presently, only Cocker, English Cocker, and English Springer Spaniels are eligible to compete in field trials.

FLYBALL

Is your puppy an athletic, active dog

with a special affinity for tennis balls? If so, flyball may be the right sport for you and your buddy. Flyball is a relay race between two teams, each with four dogs and four handlers. Each dog takes a turn running over a course with four jumps and a flyball box at the end of the course. The dog presses a pedal on the front of a flyball box. This releases a throwing arm that sends a tennis ball up in the air. The dog catches the ball and runs back over the course to the starting line. Then the next dog runs. The first team to have all four dogs successfully complete the course is the winner. It is an exciting sport, and you may find that it allows your puppy to turn his abilities into a pastime that's fun for all involved. Flyball is regulated by the North American Flyball Association (NAFA).

Flyball is a great sport for active dogs, especially those who love balls. Although you can teach your puppy to fetch at a young age, you'll need to wait to participate in flyball until after his bones mature because of the jumping requirements.

FLYING DISC

Some dogs just love to play flying disc; they sleep with it, eat with it, and live to play the next game of fetch. People have taken this and developed a sport that allows dogs to display their amazing athletic aptitude. It all started in the mid-1970s when Alex Stein ran out on the field in the middle of a Dodgers baseball game

and performed with his dog, Ashley Whippet. A nationwide audience got to enjoy the high-flying

You can familiarize your puppy with a flying disc, but leave the jumping until he's matured.

demonstration on television, and the sport of flying disc was born.

Both mixed-breed and purebred dogs can compete, but dogs who excel at flying disc are medium-sized, lean, agile dogs who are able to take flying leaps and use their owners as launching pads. Other characteristics that make a good disc dog are strong retrieving and tracking instincts, an even temperament, and sound hips.

Flying disc competitions are held all over the country. They are divided into beginner and intermediate levels, each consisting of two different events. The first event is called the mini-distance, which is played on a 20-yard (18 m) field. Competitors are given 60 seconds to make as many throws and catches as possible. The second event is the free-flight event that consists of a choreographed series of acrobatic moves to music. Judges award points on a one to ten scale in each of the following categories: degree of difficulty, execution, leaping agility, and showmanship. Bonus points can be given to competitors with spectacular or innovative free-flight moves.

Competition is regulated by organizations including the International Disc Dog Handlers Association (IDDHA) and the Flying Disc Dog Organization (FDDO).

This is a very athletic sport, and you must make sure that your puppy's body is healthy enough to participate. Although you can familiarize your puppy with a flying disc from a very young age, you should not participate in the sport until his bones are mature.

HERDING TRIALS

If your breed is in the Herding Group (or is a Samoyed or Rottweiler), you may have noticed your dog circling or "rounding up" bicycles, birds, or even your children. This inherent ability to control livestock can be put to good use by participating in herding tests and/or trials. Herding trials are designed to allow your dog to demonstrate the ability to herd under the direction of a handler. Your puppy must be at least nine months old and one of the following breeds to be eligible: Australian Cattle Dog, Australian Shepherd, Bearded Collie, Belgian Malinois, Belgian Sheepdog, Belgian Tervuren, Border Collie, Bouvier des Flandres, Briard, Canaan Dog, Cardigan Welsh Corgi, Collie, German Shepherd Dog, Old English Sheepdog, Puli, Shetland Sheepdog, Pembroke Welsh Corgi, Samoyed, or Rottweiler.

In herding trials, your dog will be judged against a set of standards and can earn advanced titles and championships by competing against other dogs for placements. Livestock used at the trials include sheep, cattle, ducks, or goats. The titles offered are HS (Herding Started), HI (Herding

Intermediate), and HX (Herding Excellent). Upon the completion of an HX, a herding championship may be earned after accumulating 15 championship points. There are also noncompetitive herding clinics and instinct tests given by AKC clubs across the country.

LURE COURSING

There is nothing more exciting than seeing your dog do what he was bred to do, especially if that dog is a sighthound racing at full speed. Lure coursing is an event in which dogs follow an artificial lure around a course on an open field. They are scored on speed, enthusiasm, agility, endurance, and their ability to follow the lure. Eligible breeds are the Afghan Hound, Basenji, Borzoi, Greyhound,

Lure coursing lets this Ibizan Hound show off his speed.

Ibizan Hound, Irish Wolfhound, Pharaoh Hound, Rhodesian Ridgeback, Saluki, Scottish Deerhound, and Whippet.

OBEDIENCE

You may find that your puppy aced puppy kindergarten and loves to work with you practicing basic commands. If you have a "workaholic" pup on your hands, obedience may be the right event for you.

Obedience trials test your dog's ability to perform a particular set of exercises. The handler and dog team is scored on performance. In each exercise, you must score more than 50 percent of the possible points (ranging from 20 to 40) and get a total score of at least 170 out of a possible 200. Each time you do this, your dog gets a "leg" toward a title. Three legs under three different judges and your dog earns an obedience title.

There are three title levels, and each is more difficult than the one before. You may see levels divided into "A" and "B"; "A" classes are for beginners whose dogs have never received a title, while "B" classes are for more experienced handlers. The three levels are Novice, Open, and Utility. The dogs who earn their Utility degrees can go on to compete for a UDX (Utility Dog Excellent) or OTCh. (Obedience Trial Championship).

The first level, Novice, requires the skills for a good canine companion. Dogs will have to heel both on and off leash at different speeds, come when called, stay with a group of other dogs, and stand for a simple physical exam. Dogs who qualify will earn a CD (Companion Dog) title after their names.

The second level, Open, requires many of the same exercises as in the Novice class, but off leash and for longer periods of time. There are also jumping and retrieving tasks. Dogs who qualify will earn a CDX (Companion Dog Excellent) title.

The final level, Utility, consists of more difficult exercises, including scent discrimination tasks. Dogs who qualify will earn a UD (Utility Dog) title.

TRACKING

All dogs love to use their noses to communicate with people and other dogs every day. Tracking tests allow dogs to demonstrate their natural ability to recognize and follow scent. This vigorous outdoor activity is especially great for canine athletes who have an affinity

Tracking

A good way to get your dog started in tracking is to play hide-and-seek in the house. Begin with the name of a certain toy that your dog likes, such as a ball. First, hide the ball, but let the dog see where you put it. Then say, "Find it." After the dog gets the hang of it, put him in another room while you hide the object. You can make the game increasingly difficult by using different objects. If your pet enjoys playing hide-and-seek, you probably have a natural tracking dog on your hands.

for tracking, such as some dogs in the Hound Group. Unlike obedience, your dog only has to pass one tracking test in order to earn this title.

There are three titles that a dog can earn in tracking events. The first is the TD or Tracking Dog title. Dogs can earn a TD by following a track laid down by a human 30 minutes to 2 hours before. The rules describe certain turns in a 440- to 500-yard (402- to 457-m) track. The second title, TDX, or Tracking Dog Excellent, is earned by following an older (laid down three to five hours before) and longer

All dogs love to use their noses.

(800 to 1,000 yards [731 to 914 m]) track with more turns while overcoming both physical and scenting obstacles. A dog who has earned a VST or Variable Surface Tracking title has demonstrated the ability to track through urban and wilderness settings by successfully following a three- to-five hour-old track that may go down a street, through buildings, or through other areas devoid of vegetation.

17

THE
AMBITIOUS
PUPPY

f dog sports isn't for you, there are many other types of activities, from therapy and assistance work to just plain having fun, that you can participate in. Determine what kinds of activities your puppy is suited to and match those abilities to your interests. This way, both you and your canine friend are guaranteed to have lots of fun together.

ACTIVITIES

Not all dog sports have to be organized events. Your puppy will be happy to join you and your family in almost any activity. Dogs thrive on exercise and will be happy to accompany you jogging, walking, or bicycling. Some breeds, like Newfoundlands and retrievers, make exceptional swimmers and can be trained for water rescue. Others will enjoy camping, backpacking, and hiking—whatever recreation you are interested in, there is a dog who can do it.

As with any form of exercise, make sure your dog is warmed up first and builds stamina slowly. Of course, you can't expect a Chihuahua to accompany you on a 10-mile (16-km) run, so also take into consideration any physical limitations. Hopefully, you have chosen your puppy with this in mind. If you take the proper precautions, your dog can be in the best physical shape—like any conditioned athlete—and you will have a great workout companion.

Hiking and Camping

If you enjoy hiking or camping, your puppy can be a great companion. Because you will be in public places

Before camping or hiking with your puppy, make sure that you understand all the rules for the place you'll be visiting.

where sick dogs may have been and where wildlife lives, your puppy must have all his shots before you take him hiking or camping. For camping alone, your puppy doesn't have to reach full maturity, but if you want him to hike or carry a backpack, wait until his bones are mature, or you could cause him injury. As always, before any physical activity it's important to get your puppy a thorough veterinary checkup to ensure that he's in good health and is a good candidate for the activity. It's best to start out with short trips and gradually work up to longer ones to increase his stamina and gradually get him used to the exercise and experience.

Before camping or hiking with your puppy, make sure that you understand all the rules for the place you'll be visiting. Some trails and campsites do not allow dogs. Read books on how to hike or camp with your puppy so that you can learn more about what to expect and what problems and dangers to avoid.

Puppies who hike or camp must have excellent manners. They will be exposed to different people and be expected to behave themselves at campsites and not disturb your fellow campers. Teach your puppy to walk politely on leash, and make sure that he has plenty of positive socialization experiences so that he will be confident and friendly in new surroundings. Also, work on your housetraining so that he learns to potty on cue. You don't want to have to walk

a long distance just waiting for your puppy to find the "perfect spot" to relieve himself. If he has a barking problem, work on that before your trip. Remember, your puppy will be experiencing different sights and sounds on the trail and in the campsite, so he may be tempted to bark, whine, or for certain breeds, howl. If you want your dog to carry a backpack, train him to do so before your trip. Be sure to work up to greater weights gradually.

If you find that your puppy has specific issues, like pulling on leash or barking at other campers, work on those issues at home and try the activity again. Always set your puppy up to succeed. For example, if you know that your puppy is hesitant around small children, do not let a small child pet him at a campsite. And never let a mob of kids surround him—you're just setting him up for disaster. Work with a reward-based trainer to help your puppy with this and any other issue

Hiking and Camping Tips

- Be sure that your puppy is up to date on his flea and tick control medication. Check him frequently for ticks, burrs, foxtails, and the like.
- Bring your puppy's first-aid kit. Check his paw pads frequently for cuts and scrapes. Watch how the weather is affecting him. Before your trip, get contact information for the nearest veterinarian and veterinary emergency clinic at your destination.
- Take plenty of rest stops, and watch for signs of overexertion or heatstroke.
- Always keep your puppy on leash. Do not leave him tethered and unsupervised because he could get tangled around tent poles, tables, or trees.
- Always pick up after your puppy and dispose of his waste in a proper receptacle.

so that he can learn to be a wonderful hiking and camping companion.

Jogging

If you're a jogger, you may enjoy sharing that activity with your puppy. Many high-energy puppies would love to run with you, but you should wait until their bones are mature before starting any strenuous running activity with them. If you begin this athletic activity too early, your puppy could sustain injuries.

Talk with your veterinarian to see if your puppy is a good candidate for jogging. He will need to be healthy, sound, and preferably not a flat-nosed breed because they often have breathing difficulties.

When you do start, start slowly. Train your dog to run short distances, and gradually work up to longer ones. Always carry water with you for him to drink, keep

a close eye for signs of overexertion and heatstroke, and be careful of the ground that you run on. It's hotter for a dog to run on asphalt because he doesn't have shoes to protect his feet. Check his paw pads regularly for cuts or scrapes.

Until your puppy is mature enough to jog with you, train him to behave politely on leash and work on your socialization exercises. These will help you later, when he's ready to become your jogging partner.

ASSISTANCE DOGS

Some puppies can be trained to assist people with physical disabilities. They can help the blind get around independently, help the deaf hear the telephone or the doorbell, and help those confined to wheelchairs accomplish everyday activities like opening doors or getting items they need. There are special programs that screen and train these puppies, as well as foster programs for people who can take in puppies to train and socialize them until they are ready to be placed with that special person.

CANINE GOOD CITIZEN CERTIFICATE

In 1989, the American Kennel Club (AKC) initiated its now immensely popular Canine Good Citizen (CGC) program. Serving as a way to recognize and reward dogs who demonstrate desirable behavior in the community and who serve as role model companion dogs, the Canine Good Citizen certificate has become a sought-after distinction by many dog owners.

To participate in the CGC program,

Lyme Lights

If you go hiking or camping with your puppy, be aware that there are certain areas of the country that have a high incidence of Lyme disease. If you plan to travel to any of the following regions, talk to your veterinarian to see if a vaccination is needed for protection: Connecticut, Massachusetts, Rhode Island, Westchester and Duchess Counties in New York, northern California, Wisconsin, Michigan's upper peninsula, and northern Illinois are all areas with a high incidence of Lyme.

AKC, with a recording fee, and receive a CGC certificate for your dog.

Part One

The CGC program is a two-step process. First, the owner must sign the Responsible Dog Owners Pledge. This document attests that the dog is under the routine care of a veterinarian who will work with the owner to determine a mutually acceptable health care plan for the dog, and that the owner agrees to take care of her dog's needs for a safe environment, exercise, training, and activities that contribute to a good quality of life. The owner also agrees to model responsible dog ownership by doing things like cleaning up after her pet in public places. The owner must also agree to demonstrate a regard for the rights of others by properly managing her dog.

Part Two

The second part of the CGC program consists of the ten-step CGC test.

Test 1: Accepting a Friendly Stranger

The dog must allow a friendly stranger to approach his handler in an everyday setting. The dog should show no signs of shyness or aggression and should not jump on the stranger or break away from his handler.

Test 2: Sitting Politely for Petting

While in the company of his handler, the dog should allow a friendly stranger to touch him without showing shyness or aggression.

puppies and dogs must be old enough to have received their required immunizations.

The CGC program recognizes dogs who demonstrate desirable behavior in the community.

The AKC suggests that puppies be retested once they have reached maturity because behavior and temperament can evolve over time. You can collect information about CGC training and testing directly from the AKC and manage the training yourself. Many dog clubs and private trainers offer classes specifically designed to prepare a dog for CGC testing.

Once your puppy has passed the CGC test, send a copy of the test form to the

Test 3: Appearance and Grooming

Of course, your puppy's stunningly handsome appearance will get you off to the right start for this exercise! The evaluator checks the overall condition of the dog, including weight, cleanliness of the coat, and alertness. Using the handler's comb or brush, the evaluator lightly grooms the dog and examines his ears and feet. The handler may encourage and praise the dog throughout the exercise.

Test 4: Out for a Walk on a Loose Lead

While walking with his handler, including turning left and right and reversing direction, the dog must be attentive to the handler and respond to her movements and changes of direction. This exercise tests that the handler is in control of the dog by means other than sheer physical restraint in the form of a constantly tight leash. The handler may talk to the dog and praise him as they walk together.

Test 5: Walking Through a Crowd

The dog and handler walk around normally and pass close to at least three people (the crowd). The dog should not jump on the crowd members, strain at the leash, or show any sign of shyness or aggression.

Test 6: Sit and Down on Command; Stay in Place

At the beginning of this test, the handler places the dog on a 20-foot (6-m) line. The dog must sit and lie down on a signal from his owner. The owner may touch the dog in a way that offers gentle guidance, but she should not force him into position. The evaluator must determine that the dog has responded to the owner's signals to sit or down and has not been physically placed in a *sit* or *down*. When the dog is in either the *sit* or *down* position, the handler tells the dog to stay and walks forward, turns, and returns to the dog. The dog must remain in place until the evaluator indicates that the handler may release the dog.

Test 7: Coming When Called

At a distance of 10 feet (3 m) from the dog, the handler calls the dog to come to him. The dog must respond.

Test 8: Reaction to Another Dog

Well-socialized dogs ace this test of a dog's ability to act politely around other dogs. You and your dog approach another handler-and-dog team, stop, exchange pleasantries, and continue on your way. Your dog should show no more than a casual interest in the other dog or his handler.

Test 9: Reaction to Distraction

The evaluator presents two common distractions, like knocking over a chair, jogging past the dog, or rolling a dolly or baby stroller in front of him. The dog may show interest and curiosity in the event or be reasonably startled, but he should not panic, run away, or bark. He should show confidence and a relaxed demeanor.

Test 10: Supervised Separation

You dog must demonstrate that he can be left under the supervision of a friendly, trusted person, and still maintain his training responses and general good manners. A tester will hold your dog on his leash for three minutes while you are out of sight. The tester will not pester your dog with excessive talking or petting, but your dog must not continually bark, whine, pace, or attempt to flee.

SEARCH AND RESCUE DOGS

In almost any city, you will find a canine search and rescue unit. These dedicated handlers and their dogs go to scenes of disasters to help find survivors and victims. They also help find people who may be lost. These handler/dog teams travel great distances and give up much of their time and energy to help others. They do this for the personal sense of satisfaction that they receive, not for money or glory.

It takes a special dog and owner to devote so much of themselves to helping others. Search and rescue dogs come in all different breeds, but all have a few traits in common: athleticism, tracking ability, and perseverance. Getting your dog certified as a search and rescue dog is not easy. You must go through rigorous training exercises under the same conditions that the dog will be facing before you are allowed to actually go to work. The best way to get started is to contact your local law enforcement agency or one of the national associations to see if there are any units in your area. The next time disaster strikes, you and your dog could be helping others—and there is no greater reward of dog ownership.

Search and rescue dogs help find people who are lost.

THERAPY DOGS

If you have a puppy who loves new people and likes to get out of the house, think about becoming a therapy team. It will be incredibly rewarding for both you and your dog.

Therapy dogs visit people in hospitals, hospices, nursing homes, schools, and libraries. Some dogs help bring a light of recognition to a person with advanced Alzheimer's disease. Others sit quietly next to a child who is trying to improve her reading skills. Others participate in physical therapy sessions with people recovering from injuries.

Many dogs are just naturally gifted at this volunteer work. They seem to sense who needs a gentle snuggle and who wants to be entertained by clownishness. It's an honor to volunteer side by side with one of these gifted dogs.

Of course, therapy work isn't for every dog. Just as every person isn't cut out to

be a social worker, every dog isn't cut out to be a therapy dog. People who evaluate therapy dogs estimate that about 25 to 30 percent of trained dogs enjoy this work. No one wants to be visited by a dog who doesn't like them, so if your dog is grouchy with strangers, he may need more training. If he has health problems that make touch uncomfortable for him, or if he's shy, this probably isn't the activity for him.

It's also important to find the right niche for each dog. Some puppies love kids but find older adults boring. Others clearly love to snuggle with older folks but find the less predictable antics of children intimidating. If you work through an animal-assisted therapy group, you and your dog will find a niche you can both enjoy.

Getting Certified as a Therapy Dog

Certification for all therapy dogs starts out with a Canine Good Citizen test, which we discussed earlier in this chapter. The certifying therapy dog organization may modify the test somewhat. For example, all organizations use wheelchairs and walkers during the "walking through a crowd" section of the test, to be sure prospective therapy dogs are comfortable around medical equipment. But some organizations don't require the supervised separation segment of the test because therapy dogs should always stay on leash with their human partners during therapy visits.

Some organizations also add extensive temperament testing to their requirements. These tests are designed to make sure your prospective therapy dog not only accepts the kinds of challenges he's likely to face in a therapy visit

If your puppy loves kids, he may find therapy work with children enjoyable.

Why Be Certified?

You have a great little dog—but it does cost some money and some time to be evaluated and certified by one of the therapy organizations. Thinking of skipping the test? Don't. Most hospitals, nursing homes, and schools require you to be certified.

Plus, the certifying organizations give their therapy dog teams liability insurance of $1 million or more as part of your membership. You must have liability coverage if you do this kind of work.

but will also actually enjoy them. The requirements of the Delta Society test are good ones to practice, no matter which organization certifies you. If you spend much time in any facility, this test evaluates your dog for his response to the following situations:

1. Overall exam (accepting handling)
2. Exuberant and clumsy petting
3. Restraining hug
4. Staggering, gesturing individual
5. Angry yelling
6. Bumped from behind
7. Crowded and petted by several people
8. Leave It (ignore a toy on the floor)
9. Offered a treat (to take gently)

No matter what you and your puppy eventually decide to do, you will have the joy of knowing that you are doing it together. As long as your puppy is well loved, there is nothing you both can't accomplish.

RESOURCES

BREED CLUBS

American Kennel Club (AKC)
5580 Centerview Drive
Raleigh, NC 27606
Telephone: (919) 233-9767
Fax: (919) 233-3627
E-mail: info@akc.org
www.akc.org

Canadian Kennel Club (CKC)
200 Ronson Drive, Suite 400
Etobicoke, Ontario
M9W 6R4
Canada
Telephone: (416) 675-5511
Fax: (416) 675-6506
E-mail: information@ckc.ca
www.ckc.ca

The Fédération Cynologique Internationale (FCI)
[World Canine Organization]
13 Place Albert 1er
B-6530 Thuin
Belgium
Telephone: 32 71 59 12 38
Fax: 32 71 59 22 29
E-mail: info@fci.be
www.fci.be

The Kennel Club
1-5 Clarges Street
Picadilly, London
W1J 8AB
United Kingdom
Telephone: 0844 463 3980
Fax: 020 7518 1058
www.thekennelclub.org.uk

United Kennel Club (UKC)
100 E. Kilgore Road
Kalamazoo, MI 49002-5584
Telephone: (269) 343-9020
Fax: (269) 343-7037
www.ukcdogs.com

ORGANIZATIONS

Animal Welfare and Rescue

American Humane Association (AHA)
63 Inverness Drive East
Englewood, CO 80112
Telephone: (800) 227-4645
Fax: (303) 792-5333
www.americanhumane.org

American Society for the Prevention of Cruelty to Animals (ASPCA)
424 E. 92nd Street
New York, NY 10128-6804
Telephone: (212) 876-7700
www.aspca.org

Canadian Federation of Humane Societies (CFHS)
102-30 Concourse Gate
Ottawa, ON K2E 7V7
Canada
Telephone: (888) 678-CFHS
Fax: (613)723-0252
E-mail: info@cfhs.ca
www.cfhs.ca

The Humane Society of the United States (HSUS)
2100 L Street, NW
Washington, DC 20037
Telephone: (202) 452-1100
www.humanesociety.org

Partnership for Animal Welfare
P.O. Box 1074
Greenbelt, MD 20768
Telephone: (301) 572-4729
E-mail: dogs@paw-rescue.org
www.paw-rescue.org

Royal Society for the Prevention of Cruelty to Animals (RSPCA)
Wilberforce Way
Southwater, Horsham,
West Sussex RH13 9RS
United Kingdom
Telephone: 0300 123 4555
Fax: 0303 123 0100
vetfone: 0906 500 5500
www.rspca.org.uk

Behavior

American College of Veterinary Behaviorists (ACVB)
Dr. Bonnie V. Beaver, ACVB

Executive Director
Texas A&M University
College Station, TX 77843-4474
E-mail: info@dacvb.org
www.veterinarybehaviorists.org

Animal Behavior Society (ABS)
Indiana University
402 N. Park Ave.
Bloomington, IN 47408-2603
Telephone: (812) 856-5541
Fax: (812) 856-5542
E-mail: aboffice@indiana.edu
www.animalbehaviorsociety.org

GROOMING

The International Society of Canine Cosmetologists (ISCC)
2702 Covington Drive
Garland, TX 75040
Fax: (972) 530-3313
E-mail: iscc@petstylist.com
www.petstylist.com

National Dog Groomers Association of America, Inc. (NDGAA)
P.O. Box 101
Clark, PA 16113
Telephone: (724) 962-2711
Fax: (724) 962-1919
E-mail: ndgaa@
nationaldoggroomers.com
www.nationaldoggroomers.com

HEALTH

The American Animal Hospital Association (AAHA)
12575 W. Bayaud Ave.
Lakewood, CO 80228
Telephone: (303) 986-2800
Fax: (303) 986-1700
E-mail: info@aahanet.org
www.aahanet.org

American Kennel Club Canine Health Foundation (AKCCHF)
P.O. Box 37941
Raleigh, NC 27627-7941
Telephone: (888) 682-9696
E-mail: caninehealth@akcchf.org
www.akcchf.org

Canine Health Information Center (CHIC)

2300 E. Nifong Blvd.
Columbia, MO 65201-3806
Telephone: (573) 442-0418
Fax: (573) 875-5073
E-mail: chic@offa.org
www.caninehealthinfo.org

Canine Eye Registration Foundation (CERF)
VMDB/CERF
1248 Lynn Hall
625 Harrison St
Purdue University
W Lafayette, IN 47907-2026
Telephone: (765) 494-8179
E-mail: CERF@vmdb.org
www.vmdb.org/cerf.html

Orthopedic Foundation for Animals, Inc. (OFA)
2300 E. Nifong Blvd.
Columbia, MO 65201-3806
Phone: (800) 442-0418
E-mail: chic@offa.org
www.offa.org

PET SITTING
The National Association of Professional Pet Sitters (NAPPS)
15000 Commerce Parkway, Suite C
Mt. Laurel, NJ 08054
Telephone: (856) 439-0324
E-mail: NAPPS@ahint.com
www.petsitters.org

Pet Sitters International
201 East King Street
King, NC 27021
Telephone: (336) 983-9222
Fax: (336) 983-5266
E-mail: info@petsit.com
www.petsit.com

PUBLICATIONS
Books
Anderson, Teoti. *Puppy Care & Training.* New Jersey: TFH Publications, Inc., 2007.

Anderson, Teoti. *The Super Simple Guide to Housetraining.* New Jersey: TFH Publications, Inc., 2004.

Boneham, Sheila Webster, Ph.D. *The Multiple-Dog Family.* New Jersey: TFH Publications, Inc., 2009.

Boneham, Sheila Webster, Ph.D. *Training Your Dog for Life.* New Jersey: TFH Publications, Inc., 2008.

Dainty, Suellen. *50 Games to Play With Your Dog.* New Jersey: TFH Publications, Inc., 2007.

DeGioia. *The Mixed Breed Dog.* New Jersey: TFH Publications, Inc., 2007.

DeVito, Russell-Revesz, Fornino. *World Atlas of Dog Breeds, 6th Ed.* New Jersey: TFH Publications, Inc., 2009.

Gagne, Tammy. *The Happy Adopted Dog.* New Jersey: TFH Publications, Inc., 2009.

Gagne, Tammy. *Living Green With Your Dog.* New Jersey: TFH Publications, Inc., 2009.

King, Trish. *Parenting Your Dog: Complete Care and Training for Every Life Stage.* New Jersey: TFH Publications, Inc., 2010.

Knueven, Doug, DVM. *The Holistic Health Guide for Dogs.* New Jersey: TFH Publications, Inc., 2008.

Mammato, Bobbie and Susie Duckworth. *Pet First Aid: Cats and Dogs.* Missouri: CV Mosby Publishing Company, 1997.

Morgan, Diane. *Feeding Your Dog for Life: The Real Facts About Proper Nutrition.* California: Doral Publishing, 2002.

Morgan, Diane. *The Living Well Guide for Senior Dogs.* New Jersey: TFH Publications, Inc., 2007.

Morgan, Diane. *Complete Guide to Dog Care (Animal Planet).* New Jersey: TFH Publications, Inc., 2011.

Magazines
AKC Family Dog
American Kennel Club
260 Madison Avenue
New York, NY 10016
Telephone: (800) 490-5675
E-mail: familydog@akc.org
www.akc.org/pubs/familydog

AKC Gazette
American Kennel Club
260 Madison Avenue
New York, NY 10016
Telephone: (800) 533-7323
E-mail: gazette@akc.org
www.akc.org/pubs/gazette

Dog & Kennel
Pet Publishing, Inc.
7-L Dundas Circle
Greensboro, NC 27407
Telephone: (336) 292-4047
Fax: (336) 292-4272
E-mail: info@petpublishing.com
www.dogandkennel.com

Dog Fancy
P.O. Box 6050
Mission Viejo, CA 92690-6050
Telephone: (800) 365-4421
E-mail: barkback@dogfancy.com
www.dogfancy.com

Dog World
P.O. Box 6050
Mission Viejo, CA 92690-6050
Telephone: (800) 365-4421
E-mail: dogworld@dogworldmag.com
www.dogworld.com

Dogs Monthly
Ascot House
29 High Street, Ascot
Berkshire, SL5 7JG
United Kingdom
Telephone: 1344 628 269
Fax: 1344 622 771
E-mail: admin@rtcassociates.freeserve.co.uk
www.corsini.co.uk/dogsmonthly

SPORTS

Agility Association of Canada (AAC)
RR#2
Lucan, Ontario N0N 2J0
Canada
Telephone: (519) 657-7636
www.aac.ca

North American Dog Agility Council (NADAC)
P.O. Box 1206
Colbert, OK 74733
E-mail: info@nadac.com
www.nadac.com

North American Flyball Association (NAFA)
1400 West Devon Avenue, #512
Chicago, IL 60660
Telephone/Fax: (800) 318-6312
E-mail: flyball@flyball.org
www.flyball.org

United States Dog Agility Association (USDAA)
P.O. Box 850955
Richardson, TX 75085-0955
Telephone: (972) 487-2200
Fax: (972) 231-9700
E-mail: info@usdaa.com
www.usdaa.com

THERAPY

The Bright and Beautiful Therapy Dogs, Inc.
80 Powder Mill Road
Morris Plains, NJ 07950
Telephone: (888) PET-5770
Fax: (973) 292-9559
E-mail: info@golden-dogs.org
www.golden-dogs.org

Delta Society Pet Partners Program
875 124th Ave. NE, Suite 101
Bellevue, WA 98005
Telephone: (425) 679-5500
Fax: (425) 679-5539
E-mail: info@deltasociety.org
www.deltasociety.org

Therapy Dogs Incorporated
P.O. Box 20227
Cheyenne, WY 82003
Telephone: (877) 843-7364
E-mail: therapydogsinc@qwestoffice.net
www.therapydogs.com

Therapy Dogs International
88 Bartley Square
Flanders, NJ 07836
Telephone: (973) 252-9800
Fax: (973) 252-7171
E-mail: tdi@gti.net
www.tdi-dog.org

TRAINING

Association of Pet Dog Trainers (APDT)
101 North Main St., Suite 610
Greenville, SC 29601
Telephone: (800) PET-DOGS
Fax: (864) 331-0767
E-mail: information@apdt.com
www.apdt.com

Certification Council for Pet Dog Trainers (CCPDT)
1350 Broadway, 17th Floor
New York, NY 10018
Telephone: (212) 356-0682
E-mail: administrator@ccpdt.org
www.ccpdt.org

VETERINARY

Academy of Veterinary Homeopathy (AVH)
P.O. Box 232282
Leucadia, CA 92023-2282
Telephone/Fax: (866) 652-1590
www.theavh.com/contact/index.php

American Academy of Veterinary Acupuncture (AAVA)
P.O. Box 1058
Glastonbury, CT 06033
Telephone: (860) 632-9911
Fax: (860) 659-8772
E-mail: office@aava.org
www.aava.org

American Animal Hospital Association (AAHA)
12575 W. Bayaud Ave.
Lakewood, CO 80228
Telephone: (303) 986-2800
Fax: (303) 986-1700
E-mail: info@aahanet.org
www.aahanet.org

American College of Veterinary Internal Medicine (ACVIM)
1997 Wadsworth Blvd., Suite A
Lakewood, CO 80214-5293
Telephone: (800) 245-9081
Fax: (303) 231-0880
E-mail: ACVIM@ACVIM.org
www.acvim.org.

American College of Veterinary Ophthalmologists (ACVO)
P.O. Box 1311
Meridian, ID 83680
Telephone: (208) 466-7624
Fax: (208) 466-7693
E-mail: office10@acvo.org
www.acvo.org

American Holistic Veterinary Medical Association (AHVMA)
2218 Old Emmorton Road
Bel Air, MD 21015
Telephone: (410) 569-0795
Fax: (410) 569-2346
E-mail: office@ahvma.org
www.ahvma.org

American Veterinary Chiropractic Association (AVCA)
442154 E 140 Road
Bluejacket, OK 74333
Telephone: (918) 784-2231
Fax: (918) 784-2675
E-mail: avcainfo@junct.com
www.animalchiropractic.org

American Veterinary Dental Society (AVDS)
P.O. Box 803
Fayetteville, TN 37334
Telephone: (800) 332-AVDS
Fax: (931) 433-6289
E-mail: avds@avds-online.org
www.avds-online.org

American Veterinary Medical Association (AVMA)
1931 North Meacham Road, Suite 100
Schaumburg, IL 60173-4360
Telephone: (800) 248-2862
Fax: (847) 925-1329
E-mail: avmainfo@avma.org
www.avma.org

International Veterinary Acupuncture Society (IVAS)
1730 South College Ave., Suite 301
Ft. Collins, CO 80527-1395
Telephone: (970) 266-0666
Fax: (970) 266-0777
E-mail: office@ivas.org
www.ivas.org

US Food & Drug Administration's Center for Veterinary Medicine (CVM)
Communications Staff (CVM)
Food and Drug Administration
7519 Standish Place, HFV-12
Rockville, MD 20855
Telephone: (240) 276-9300
E-mail: ASKCVM@fda.hhs.gov
www.fda.gov/cvm/default.htm

Veterinary Cancer Society (VCS)
P.O. Box 1763
Spring Valley, CA 91979
Telephone: (619) 741-2210
Fax: (619) 741-1117
E-mail: vcs@cox.net
www.vetcancersociety.org

WEBSITES

General

Animal Planet
www.animal.discovery.com
The domestic dog section has a great guide to dogs, a breed selector, training information, and more.

Nylabone®
www.nylabone.com
Nylabone premium chews, toys, and other products promote good canine dental hygiene, enhance overall mental fitness, encourage positive behavior, provide comfortable shelter, and allow for safe, pleasant travel.

TFH Publications, Inc.
www.tfh.com
Comprehensive and authoritative animal reference books and learning vehicles for pet owners that ensure the optimum human–companion animal experience.

Activities

Carting With Your Dog
www.cartingwithyourdog.com
Information and resources on carting.

DogPlay
www.dogplay.com
Excellent guide to activities that you can do with your dog.

Dog Works, Inc.
www.dogworks.com
A great source for canine carting and watersports equipment.

Hike With Your Dog
www.hikewithyourdog.com
Direct links to more than 2,000 dog-friendly parks, plus dog regulations for national parks in the US and Canada.

Skyhoundz
www.skyhoundz.com
Products and events for disc dog enthusiasts.

Sled Dog Central
www.sleddogcentral.com
Sled dog information resource.

SportsVet.com
http://www.sportsvet.com
Website dedicated to athletic and working dogs. A great site for health and care information for your canine athlete.

Behavior

Pet Behavior Resources
www.webtrail.com/petbehavior
A guide to all aspects of pet behavior.

Dumb Friends League
www.ddfl.org
Excellent advice for solving common pet behavioral problems.

Legal

American Dog Owner's Association
www.adoa.org
Information and ideas about preserving dog owners' rights, and information about responsible dog ownership.

Animal Legal Defense Fund
www.aldf.org
Advancing the lives of animals through the legal system.

Dog Watch
www.dogwatch.net
Provides information on canine breed-specific legislation in North America and abroad.

National Animal Interest Alliance
www.naiaonline.org
Provides expert information on animals and public policy.

NUPP Legal
www.nupplegal.com/pets.html
Legal form for pet owners who are renting is available for purchase on this website.

People With Pets
www.peoplewithpets.com
A free nationwide apartment locator service for people with pets.

Lost and Missing Pets

Last Chance for Animals
www.stolenpets.com
Learn about how to combat the problem of stolen pets who are sold to research institutions.

Missing Pet Network
www.missingpet.net
Website run by a group of volunteers sponsored by the USDA Animal Care Office, who help people find missing pet animals.

Pets 911
www.pets911.org
Contains a nationwide list of animal control facilities, humane societies, and veterinarians; searchable by zip code.

Medical

Dog Genome Project
www.fhcrc.org/science/dog_
genome
A collaborative study aimed
at producing a map of all the
chromosomes in dogs.

Pet Dental
www.petdental.com
Provides information about proper
oral health care for dogs and cats.

Vetinfo
www.vetinfo.com/dogindex.html
An alphabetical listing and
discussion of dog illnesses.

Special Needs

Deaf Dog Education Action Fund
www.deafdogs.org
Provides education and funding for
the purpose of improving and saving
the lives of deaf dogs.

K-9 Carts
www.k9carts.com
Manufacturer of "K-9 Carts,"
wheelchairs for mobility-impaired
pets.

Owners of Blind Dogs
www.blinddogs.com
Provides support and information to
blind dogs and their owners.

Webzines

Dog Owner's Guide
www.canismajor.com/dog
A free online magazine that contains
sections on choosing a dog, breed
profiles, nutrition, health, training,
travel, sports, and rescue.

Bark Bytes
www.barkbytes.com
Canine cyber magazine featuring
breed profiles and many links.

Working Dogs Cyberzine
www.workingdogs.com
An international magazine for and
about working and sporting dogs.

INDEX

Boldfaced numbers indicate illustrations.

consequences, 181, 182
consistency, 160, 181, 183
copper toxicosis, 131
coprophagia, 201–202
core vaccines, 104
Corgis, 18, 20
coronavirus, 106
coughing, 116
CPR, 122, 123
crates, 76–77
    collars and, 76
    don'ts for, 173
    housetraining with, 174
    location of, 171–172, **172**
    size of, 171
    time limits in, 171
    time-out in, 170
    travel in, 210, 211–212
crate training, 170–173
crying, 114–115
cuts or wounds, 115

D

Dachshund, 23, 226–227
Dalmatian, 25, 27
dancing with dogs, 224
deciduous teeth, 148–149, 200, 201
Delta Society, 240, 241
demodectic mange, 108
dental care, **148**, 148–150
dermatitis, fleabite, 109
development, 158–163
    sporting activities and, 220, 224
    tooth, 148–149
diarrhea, 115, 130
diet sheet, 91–92, 138. *See also* feeding; food
digging, **202**, 202–204, **203**
discipline, 159, 160
distemper, 90, 103, 105, 106
distractions, eliminating, 187
Doberman Pinscher, 47
dog breeds. *See* breeds
dog food. *See* feeding; food
dog ownership, 8–9
    lifestyle and, 11–12
    space for, 9–11
    time for, 9
dog run, 85
dogs, other, 95, **95**, 165, 166, **167**
Dogue de Bordeaux, 47
doors, open, 83
down command, 184, 192
draft work, 224, **225**
drowning, 123
dry food, 134

E

ear care, 150–151, **151**
ears, healthy, 68, 100
earth dog, 34
earthdog trials, 225
electrical wires, 82
electrocution, 123
eliminating, crying when, 114. *See also* housetraining
emergency situations, 120–127
English Cocker Spaniel, 30
English Springer Spaniel, 31
escape artist, 199–200, **200**
exercise. *See also* activities; sports and events
    precautions for, 234
    requirements for, 13, **13**, 52
exercise pen, 77
eye care, 151–152
eye contact, 184–185
eye medication, 116
eye problems, 57, 115, 116
eyes, healthy, 68, 100, **115**

F

fainting, 115
fat, dietary, 132
fear, 164, 166–167, 204–205
fearful posture, 163
fear periods, 90, 159, 161
feces, eating, 201–202
feeding, 130–141. *See also* food
    amount for, 139–140
    breed-specific needs for, 130–132
    commercial foods for, 134–137
    diet sheet for, 91–92, 138
    do's and don'ts of, 141
    essential nutrients for, 130–132, 134, **135**
    homemade diets for, 137–138
    housetraining and, 175
    schedule for, 93, 138–139, **139**
    supplements for, 140
    travel and, 213, 217, **217**
    treats and bones for, 140
    vegetarian diet for, 133
    veterinary advice on, 102–103
female puppies, 66, 112–113
fences, 84
field events, **226**, 226–227
"find it," 230
first aid, 120–127
first-aid kit, 120
fleas, 108–109
flyball, 227
flying disc, 227–228, **228**
Flying Disc Dog Organization (FDDO), 228
food, 79–80. *See also* feeding
    changing type of, 80, 92, 138
    commercial, 134
    reading labels on, 134–137
    refusing, 115–116
    training with, 139, 182

PHOTOS

Isabelle Francias: 5, 17 (bottom), 18 (middle), 21 (top), 22 (bottom), 23 (top, middle), 30 (top and top inset), 31 (top and bottom), 32 (middle), 33 (middle), 35 (bottom inset), 37 (top and top inset), 38 (bottom), 39 (top), 43 (bottom inset), 44 (top and middle inset, top), 50 (bottom inset), 59, 61, 64, 73, 103, 153, 154 (center), 207 (center), 215, 221

Amy McCrary, 148

Jean M. Fogle, 229

Courtesy of www.shutterstock.com:

Eric Lam, 1, 32 (middle inset), 42 (middle), 48 (middle), 49 (top inset); Eric Isselee, 3 (top), 18 (top and top inset), 23 (bottom), 26 (bottom), 27 (bottom), 28 (top inset), 30 (bottom inset), 34 (top and top inset), 37 (middle), 39 (bottom), 40 (middle), 42 (bottom), 44 (middle), 45 (top inset), 47 (bottom inset), 48 (bottom inset), 49 (middle inset), 52 (top), 53, 56, 94, 125, 126, 160, 161; Geir Olav Lyngfjell, 3 (second from top); Tad Denson, 3 (third from top); Monica Wisniewska, 3 (second from bottom); Gelpi, 3 (bottom), 72, 198; Dmitry Kalinovsky, 4, 152; Waldemar Dabrowski, 5 (middle), 25 (top inset), 50 (top), 87, 156; Leslie Murray, 6; FotoJagodka, 8, 45 (bottom), 52 (top inset); pixshots, 10, 144; Kelly Richardson, 11; Shirelle Reggio-Manning, 12; Andrezej Mielcarek, 13; Mariusz Szachowski, 14, 82; Stas Volik, 17 (top inset); Lee O'Dell, 17 (top); vgm, 17 (middle inset), 67; Zuzule, 17 (middle), 18 (bottom), 19 (middle), 30 (bottom), 32 (bottom), 33 (bottom inset), 51 (top); cynoclub, 17 (bottom inset), 18 (middle), 19 (middle inset), 24 (bottom), 46 (bottom), 50 (top inset, middle), 57; Degtyaryov Andrey, 18 (bottom inset); Christian Mueller, 19 (top); Aleksey Ignalenko, 19 (top inset); Aorgeir Amarsson, 19 (bottom); Gleb Semenjuk, 19 (bottom inset); Pedro Jorge Henriques, 20 (top); Svetlana Valoueva, 20 (top inset), 32 (bottom inset), 36 (middle inset), 47 (top inset), 51 (middle); Andrew Chin, 20 (middle); Reddogs, 20 (middle inset); Mary Ann Kahn, 20 (bottom); Lenkadan, 20 (bottom inset), 28 (bottom inset), 30 (middle inset), 39 (bottom inset); Jerzy, 21 (top inset); Aneta Pics, 21 (bottom inset), 27 (top and bottom inset), 33 (top inset), 45 (bottom inset), 49 (middle), 51 (top inset); Mariusz Szachowski, 21 (bottom); Patricia Plunkett, 22 (top); Art_Man, 22 (top inset), 111, 237; Rhonda

ODonnell, 22 (middle); Peter Kirillov, 22 (middle inset), 226; Greenfire, 22 (bottom inset); B&T Media Group Inc, 23 (top inset), 29 (bottom inset); alexan55, 23 (middle inset); Utekhina Anna, inset (bottom), 41 (top, middle inset), 46 (top); Dee Hunter, 24 (top); Marina Jay, 24 (top inset), 28 (bottom); ncn18, 24 (middle); karloss, 24 (middle inset); Laila Kazakevica, 24 (bottom inset); Medvedev Andrey, 25 (top); Connie Wade, 25 (bottom inset); Ron Rowan Photography, 25 (bottom); WilleeCole, 26 (top inset and top), 43 (bottom), 79, 136, 147, 187; pavelmayorov, 26 (top inset); Paul Cotney, 26 (middle); YAN WEN, 26 (bottom inset), 47 (middle inset); Annette Kurka, 27 (top); david woodberry Pure Eye Photo, 27 (middle); Natalia V Guseva, 27 (middle inset), 38 (top inset); Ruth Black, 28 (top); Milan Vachal, 28 (middle inset); Malota, 28 (middle); @erics, 29 (top inset); shutterstock.com, 29 (bottom), 40 (top inset), 54, 75, 92, 116, 141, 155; Joy Brown, 30 (middle), 33 (bottom inset), 78, 112, 120, 131, 138, 200; Ken Hurst, 31 (top inset); Linn Currie, 31 (middle inset), 41 (top inset), 188; jllingebiel, 31 (middle); eAlisa, 31 (bottom inset), 37 (bottom); Joop Snijder jr., 32 (top inset), 137; Dan Flake, 32 (top); vgm, 33 (top); Barna Tanko, 33 (middle inset); Mikulich Alexander Andrevich, 34 (bottom); Claudia Steininger, 35 (top inset); Anyka, 35 (top), 194, 201, 214; eleana, 35 (middle inset), 41 (middle); Jan de Wild, 35 (middle); PHB.cz (Richard Semik), 35 (bottom), 217; Elisabeth Ahmmerschmid, 36 (top); pio3, 36 (top inset); Rybin, 36 (middle); mariait, 36 (bottom); Gina Callaway, 36 (bottom inset); Sandra Zuerlein, 37 (middle inset); Ninelle, 37 (bottom inset); Denis Babenko, 38 (top); Jacqueline Abromeit, 38 (middle), 118; marilyn barbone, 38 (middle inset); Steven Pepple, 38 (bottom inset); Sally Wallis, 39 (top inset); Marcel Jancovic, 40 (top), 84; Peter Kirillov, 40 (middle); Viorel Sima, 40 (bottom); Dorottya Mathe, 40 (bottom inset); Sergey Lavrentev, 41 (bottom inset), 207, 220, 241; Jim Larson, 41 (bottom); luchschen, 42 (top); Alexandr Ryzhov, 42 (top inset); Degtyarov Andrey Leonidovich, 42 (middle inset); Bajji, 42 (bottom inset); Alexia Kruscheva, 43 (top inset); Katrina Brown, 43 (top), 51 (bottom); Liliya Kulianionak, 43 (middle), 88; Ksenia Merenkova, 43 (middle inset); Sergey Lavrentev, 44 (bottom inset); dien, 44 (bottom); simu, 45 (top); uabels, 46 (top inset); guillermo77, 46 (middle inset); Vitaly Titov & Marina Sidelnilova, 46 (bottom), 70, 76; Vladimir

Mucibabic, 47 (top); Nikolai Tsvetkov, 47 (middle), 202; minik, 47 (bottom); Volker Hopf, 48 (top); leli, 48, (top inset); s-eyerkaufer, 48 (middle inset); deniss09, 48 (bottom); Christian Mueller, 49 (top), 91; Crystal Kirk, 49 (bottom), 184; Susan Schmitz, 50 (middle inset); Liliya Kulianionak, 50 (bottom); DM_Cherry, 51 (middle inset); hunta, 51 (bottom inset); seiseis, 58; Amy Chiara Allen, 60; DD Photography, 62; Nikolai Tsvetkov, 63 (bottom); Jamie Hewitson, 63 (top); Andresr, 66; pixel-pets, 69; Donald Joski, 77; Scott T Slattery, 81; Jesse Kunerth, 83; Golden Pixels LLC, 86; hannamariah, 95, 108; Cynthia Kidwell, 96; Michelle D Milliman, 96-97; Ljupco Smokovski, 97; Dumitrescu Ciprian-Florin, 98; Monika Wisniewska, 100; IKO, 102; Robert Adrian Hillman, 105; Alice Mary Herden Vision-Vault LLC, 107; MAGDALENA SZACHOWSKA, 114; AI vision, 115; Lars Christensen, 122; Joanna Zopoth-Lipiejko, 124; IrinaK, 128; Scorpp, 132, 142; Cynthia Kidwell, 135; Rick's Photography, 139;

Lusoimages, 145; Sean MacLeay, 151; joyfull, 154; Suponev Vladimir, 158; Micimakin, 162; Mars Evis, 165; Jesse Kunerth, 167; Glen Jones, 168; Bianca Lagalla, 172; SueC, 174; Nancy Hixson, 176; Glenkar, 177; Sharon Morris, 178; MAGDALENA SZACHOWSKA, 181; Ostanina Ekaterina Vadimovna, 182; Anson0618, 185; Nata Sdobnikova, 190, 191; Eastimages, 193; Nagy Melinda, 196; Michael Zysman, 199; GJS, 203; Andrejs Pidjass, 204; verityjohnson, 206; Martin Valigursky, 208; Anne Kitzman, 210; Cameron Cross, 212; Natalia Sinjushina & Eugeniy Meyke, 218; Anke van Wyk, 225; George Lee, 228; JKlingebiel, 231; Caleb Foster, 232; Kato Inowe, 234; Jim Parkin, 239; teekaygee, 29 (top); Lerche&Johnson, 49 (bottom inset)

Cover: Eric Lam (Shutterstock.com)

Back Cover: Stefan Petru Adronache (Shutterstock.com)

Flap: Eric Isselee (Shutterstock.com)

ACKNOWLEDGEMENTS

We would like to thank the following pet-care experts for their contributions:

Teoti Anderson, CPDT-KA; Diane Morgan; Lexiann Grant; Shelia Webster Boneham, Ph.D.; Susan M. Ewing; Janice Biniok; Tammy Gagne; Phyllis DeGioia; Deb Wood; Lorie Long; Cindy Gallagher; Elaine Gewirtz; Nikki Moustaki; Dominique De Vito; Heather Russell-Revesz; Stephanie Fornino